Financial
Maturity
AFTER.
the Recession

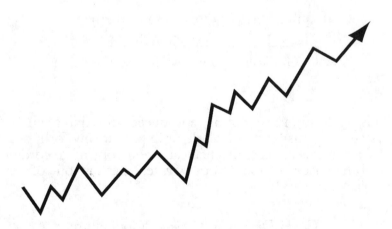

Financial Maturity After The Recession

ISBN: 9780983127055

Published by
GodKulture Scrybes
A GodKulture Company
Chicago, Illinois

Coordinating Editor: Segun Adebayo

Phone: 815-630-9890, 402-419-1072
Email: gkscrybes@Godkulture.org
www.Godkulture.org | www.gkscrybes.com

Cover Design and Layout: Godkulture

Printed in United States of America

Dedication

I dedicate this book to my late parents, Pa Augustine Ogbeni Ekhomu and Madam Cecilia Edowaye Ekhomu, who spent her life being a philanthropist.

Also to my children — Jessica, Christina, Nicole, and Aquilla.

Be wise with your finances!

To my niece — Pastor Sophia Nehita Ovonlen.

Acknowledgements

My first and foremost gratitude goes to the Holy Spirit for helping me through the fat and lean times in life, and the inspiration for this book;

Also, I am indeed grateful to all who pushed me and motivated me to write a book in my discipline and spiritual vocation. God bless you all. Specifically, I thank the Lord for the members of the Telephone Bible Study Ministry, who have been absolutely supportive of the ministry that the Lord has endowed me with since 2004;

My gratitude to my father in the faith, Pastor Leke Adesanya, of the Glorious Church of the First Born, Otukpo, Benue State, Nigeria – he kept encouraging me, even when my empire was collapsing – he stood steadfastly by my side, along with Pastor Ayo Adeloye of The Redeemed Church of the God with every word of wisdom.

To my beloved siblings; Mr. John Ekhomu, Mrs. Mary Fashanu, Dr. Augusta Ogbene, Mr. Osagie Ekhomu, Dr. Ona Ekhomu, Mrs. Christy Tometi, Mrs. Lizzy Anibueze, Pastor (Mrs.) Julie Aigbokhan for their support and constant encouragement.

Table of Contents

Foreword

And God is able to make all grace abound toward you, that you, always having all sufficiency in all things, may have an abundance for every good work.

(2 Corinthians 9:8)

It is the will of God that Christians should live a life of abundance. However, many of them are not experiencing this because of their failure to faithfully practice the covenant. We live in an imperfect, fallen world, and as a result, it is required that we live by the principles of the kingdom in order to thrive.

The Babylonian system of buying and selling which has sustained the world for the last 6000 years is now getting exhausted and falling apart. It is no longer reliable because it is a product of a fallen man. Nevertheless, God has prepared a kingdom system, which Jesus came to establish on earth, and it is imperative that we live by it.

The world is in recession today because it is not in alignment with God's ways. The system of buying and selling has been adopted in place of God's system of seedtime and harvest.

Today, a lot of people are down financially because of the world's economic crisis or as a result of their negligence. However, there is a way out of this predicament if people involved can trust God to lead them aright.

God has a superior system that He wants us to adopt so that we can dominate and occupy in this world. The corporate system of this world is not His. A lot of people are bowing down to the corporate system, forgetting and neglecting the system of God. Enough of bowing at the wrong altar! Become challenged today to move from living a low-level life to a much higher level by embracing the principles of God's kingdom.

No matter the level of financial despair you may find yourself in, now is the time to make the necessary adjustment and seek God, so that He can lead you into your Promise Land. God does not condone laziness; in fact, He wants us to be good stewards of the resources He entrusts into our hands.

This call for financial maturity and responsibility for the actions we take. Financial maturity is the ability to delay gratification. A financially mature person has a long term perspective that focuses not on the here and now, but on the future. He has the ability to give up today's desires for future benefits. He realizes that money is a resource and a tool to achieve his goals. It is not necessarily an end by itself.

For instance, a garden does not determine whether a family that owns it lives or dies. It is simply a resource that can help the family live better. Vegetables are good for preservation, but we can survive without them. Even though money is essential, it is not life, and neither is it oxygen. It is simply a tool which can be used to make ends meet. The financially mature person does work to increase its availability by making extra money and spending less on unnecessary consumption.

For all who have enough deposits in their accounts in glory through the payment of their tithes and giving of their offerings, God will supply all their needs according to His riches in glory. The proper management of these heavenly supplies is necessary. It is important that we not only benefit directly from it, but also that we be a blessing to others through it, because it is more blessed to give than to receive. This proper management can only be achieved through financial maturity.

The whole creation has been groaning together in the pains of labor until now, because the children of God are not exhibiting their divine prowess, most especially in the financial arena. Endeavor to love and seek after God, because only those who love and search for Him diligently will find Him. Not only will they find Him, He will also make enduring wealth which cannot be corrupted available to them, and give them the wisdom to manage it.

In this admirable book, Pastor Godfrey Ekhomu, a man who has been tested and proven, provides some answers to this economic impasse in details. He has done an in-depth study of why people suffer financially. But, he does not stop there; he also shows what people must do to achieve financial buoyancy for the rest of their lives.

This great work is a must read for everyone. I have no doubt that by the time you finish reading this book, you will have a new perspective on how to manage your finances wisely.

Kayode Ijisesan
Lead Pastor, KingsWord Int'l Churches

Preface

This book was written to address the need for direction, now that the recession is over. Recession is biblical famine. In the past few years, we have had to endure hostile financial conditions resulting from overspending and digging deeper in debt. At the national level, the federal government was in a financial abyss. The national debt was accelerating its way up as fast as it could; the unemployment rate rose to 10%.

The bickering between the two major political parties created a toxic atmosphere in the nation. There were those who would want to solve the problem and others who would want to talk about the problems. Employers showed much timidity and would not support the federal government. Small businesses suffered the most because banks refused to grant them credit to do business, despite pleas from President Barack Obama. All these ills trickled down to the common Jack and Jill.

Recent weeks have shown signs of hope. Businesses are beginning to hire slowly but gradually; loans are being extended to small businesses, even at a reduced rate.

The foreclosure epidemic has subsided considerably. And the rain is coming back slowly but surely. Those who have suffered through the economic woes and who were once champions of their generation are on their way back.

Although the lesson from this famine shook their faith, they believe that God has given them another chance to make it. Now that the chance is here, what should they do? That is what is being addressed in this book. Financial Maturity is attained when you follow the lead of the Holy Spirit.

This book is broken into chapters dealing with maximizing your income, budgeting, debt restructuring, philanthropic lifestyle, and contingency.

The book is called *Financial Maturity after the Recession* because of lessons learned during the recession. These lessons will bring out the best in you and help you become more mature in your financial dealings. Why? Because you know! You have experienced it, as the apostle Paul said in Romans 8:28; "*And we know that all things work together for good...*"

Be absolutely blessed,

G. O. Ekhomu
Godfrey Ekhomu, CPA

(1)

The PGE Fulfillment Model

Trust in the LORD with all thine heart; and lean not unto thine own understanding. In all thy ways acknowledge him, and he shall direct thy paths.

(Proverbs 3:5-6)

In this Chapter, you will learn about:

➤ Misalignment with God's Purpose

➤ Department of Errors and Mistakes

➤ Consequences

➤ Corrections

PGE Fulfillment Model

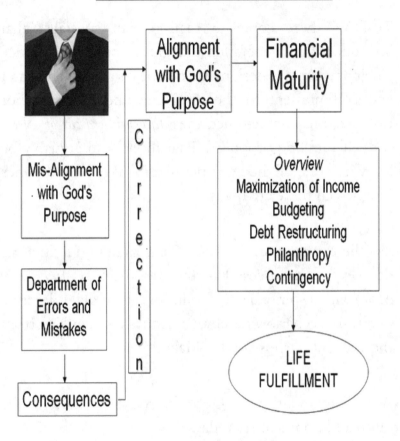

MIS-ALIGNMENT WITH GOD'S PURPOSE

TODAY there comes a management specialist that introduces their generation to a grand concept or model. Their braveness to design a model speaks to their character and commitment to the discipline under review. For instance, Maslow designed the *Maslow Hierarchy of Needs* for self-fulfilling prophesy. That model can arguably be known as one of the most popular management theories – of which there are many.

As the recession took its toll, I embarked on a doctoral degree. In the process I formulated the *PGE Fulfillment Model* with a spiritual angle to it. In the model, I describe a spiritual scenario whereby a person is disentangled from the will and purpose of his Maker.

A misalignment with God's purpose appears to be rampant in our society today.

King Solomon implored in Proverbs 3:5-6;

Trust in the LORD with all your heart, and lean not on your own understanding. In all your ways acknowledge Him, and He shall direct your paths.

The ability to understand and follow these verses of Scripture really would help one to escape complications in life. There is the constant temptation to lean on your own understanding. The reason for this is that your understanding is what you know. It is very easy to defer to what you know because it appears to be less risky in life. (Please note that leaning or deferring to what you know is not necessarily bad). It becomes bad when God is not in it. You might ask; "How do I know that God is in it?"

Firstly, I am sure you would have consulted the Holy Spirit before embarking on any venture. As you seek the Holy Spirit's help, He then illuminates the right path. The desired path of the Holy Spirit is very comforting and soothing, and so when you go in that path, you will be rest assured that He will help you and give you the necessary guidance.

Remember that the Holy Spirit is "all knowing" and as such, your venture is not new to Him. He knows the beginning and the end of all deals, and how best to make the outcome glorious.

Secondly, you have to understand the role of the Holy Spirit in your life.

According to John 6:63;

It is the spirit that quickeneth; the flesh profiteth nothing: the words that I speak unto you, [they] are spirit, and [they] are life.

So when there is a venture you are embarking on, and when you solicit the help of the Holy Spirit, He quickens the resolve. As a quickening Spirit, the Holy Spirit paves the way and pushes away all forms of obstacles. To explain further, let me use an illustration of the American football. The Holy Spirit represents the offensive linemen that help pave the way for the *Running Back*.

After the Running Back gets a paved path from the offensive linemen, he then overcomes the defensive linemen, and goes to score a touchdown. Note also that the defensive linemen are tasked to stop the Running Back - and deprive him from scoring a touchdown.

So, it is with the Holy Spirit. He pushes away the enemy and allows you the opportunity to become victorious. Therefore, when you lean on the Lord, you will get a desired positive outcome. The desired result is positive because God's plans for you are.

The Bible says in Jeremiah 29:11;

For I know the thoughts that I think toward you, says the LORD, thoughts of peace and not of evil, to give you a future and a hope.

God does not sit to think evil about you. He cannot bad mouth His own work. When He made you, He said it was good. He was so pleased about you that He gave you dominion over everything else. That's how pleased He was and He is about you. You are the apple of His eye. Every decision about you has an expected glorious end.

So when the bills come due, God has a plan - a way of escape as described by the Apostle Paul in 1 Corinthians 10:13;

No temptation has overtaken you except such as is common to man; but God is faithful, who will not allow you to be tempted beyond what you are able, but with the temptation will also make the way of escape, that you may be able to bear it.

When you drift into a porous and contaminated zone, you would find yourself misaligned from God's purpose. God is faithful and does not need your help to make His plans for you come alive. When God needs you to become involved, He will communicate that to you. When you are in a tight spot, God will make a way out of the dilemma and also help you become successful in life. God is more interested in your success than you would ever imagine. He cares about those things that pertain to you – it includes your ventures and dealings.

David wrote in Psalms 138:8;

The LORD will perfect [that which] concerneth me: thy mercy, O LORD, [endureth] for ever: forsake not the works of thine own hands.

When God perfects the works of His hands, the outcome is always very beautiful. God cannot lie because He is not a man – clearly, God cannot forsake the works of His own hands.

DEPARTMENT OF ERRORS AND MISTAKES

There is a department everyone visits in their lifetime. That is the department of errors and mistakes. This department was created because every now and then, we tend to stray. There are people who stray and there are those who stray indeed. This is separated or defined by the magnitude of their errors or mistakes. Some mistakes are very costly and could terminate the destiny of a person.

Take for instance the story of King Saul. His error terminated his destiny as a King (see the full story in 1 Samuel 15). Briefly, King Saul was given specific instructions to destroy the Amalekites due to all the evil they had brought against the children of Israel.

When Saul received instructions from Prophet Samuel, he did not reject the instructions, instead he promised the prophet that he would carry out the instructions, but failed to do so. He lied to Samuel about executing the instructions. He was caught in a lie (first by God who sees all and knows all things; secondly, by the bleating sheeps at the back of his home). The Kingdom was stripped from him and as a result, God chose David to replace him).

The second critical error committed by King Saul was consulting with the witch of Endor after the Lord refused to speak to him.

And when Saul enquired of the LORD, the LORD answered him not, neither by dreams, nor by Urim, nor by prophets; then said Saul unto his servants, Seek me a woman that hath a familiar spirit that I may go to her, and enquire of her. And his servants said to him, Behold, [there is] a woman that hath a familiar spirit at Endor."

(1 Samuel 28:6-7)

After the Lord declined to communicate with Saul, he took matters into his hands by seeking alternative way of conversing with God. Needless to say that this further damaged Saul's relationship with God, which made his day of destruction nearer.

Fundamental errors or mistakes in your life could prove to be very costly. In many cases, these mistakes can result in broken homes, failed career, bad health, and so on.

It is important to know that there are consequences for every poor judgment. Many people have taken wrong turns in life by poor choices which have haunted them. (Even) in financial terms, an error in poor investment choice could lead to a bleeding financial account.

For starters, it takes a while to build a comfortable nest egg or a good savings account. As in most cases, when you allow the spirit of greed, the nest egg evaporates into the thin air. Most people do not make a conscious decision to abuse their finances. They are pressured and enticed by the spirit of greed to do what they would not normally do.

Then they take risks that are unreasonable and have no basis. Inevitably, the outcome might be very harmful to their well-being. There are many true stories regarding this – one that comes to mind is a young man who took a sizeable amount of his 401(k) plan funds and risked it all in a more daring and risky foreign currency trade. All of the money was gone within four days of trading. This is a clear example of someone not using wisdom or following the will of God.

As stated above, relationships have been destroyed by these indiscretions and have created complications in many different ways or settings.

CONSEQUENCES

The failure to follow God's proposed plan might lead to huge embarrassing consequences in life. Let's review a few:

Poor Choices: Making a poor career choice might lead to a dead end situation in life. When a person's call is in medicine and he ends up becoming a real estate broker, he might suffer the consequences of his disobedience and would struggle through life. The failure to follow God's guidance might lead to prolonged obstacles and suffering.

In exiting Egypt, the children of Israel murmured against God several times and that lengthened their journey to the Promise Land. A journey of a few days lasted 40 years. The failure to heed God's counsel can cause broken relationships – God decrees that families should be together, but when families make poor decisions, they are torn apart and thus, God's original purpose is hindered by the hands of man.

A broken home brings forth confused children. The children are sometimes forced to choose between the parents.

Distance from God: When you fail to follow God's leading and precepts on an issue, you find yourself running and distancing yourself from God. For instance, Cain did all he could to avoid God when he murdered his brother, Abel. Whenever you avoid God and his counsel, you start to find cover in places where cover does not exist. You avoid fellowshipping with Him and make excuses for why things have not worked out for you.

CORRECTION

King Solomon said;

My son, do not despise the chastening of the LORD, Nor detest His correction; For whom the LORD loves He corrects, Just as a father the son in whom he delights.

(Proverbs 3:11-12)

Correction is a process that encourages the retracement of our ways. The Lord corrects man in order to get the best out of him. Correction normally occurs when the current path leads to destruction.

I was once told of a young man who failed to listen to every form of correction; finally not too long he ended up in jail and his record was tainted. Prior to going to jail, preachers in his locality reached out to him, offering to counsel him. He seemed to have listened, but he decided to follow his own way. He was involved with the wrong set of friends. Eventually, he and his friends were apprehended for robbing a local grocery store. His rebellious actions landed him in jail.

Correction can come through the Word of God. King David could testify to this. He had staged a grandiose coup where the husband of Bathsheba was killed by his command. After the plan had been carried out, David also took Bathsheba for a wife (See 2 Samuel 11 for the full story).

The beginning of 2 Samuel 12 reads;

Then the Lord sent Nathan unto David…

The Lord sent Prophet Nathan to David to denounce his deeds and seek correction. David's callous scheme cost Uriah his life and wife. It could be argued that King David did not realize the severity of his crime because he committed the offense under the hypnosis of lust and passion.

So, covering up his wrongdoing was just a natural phenomenon in order not to be caught. Admitting to his guilt was the turning point of David's life.

The Bible says;

So David said to Nathan, "I have sinned against the LORD." And Nathan said to David, The LORD also has put away your sin; you shall not die.

(2 Samuel 12:13)

When correction occurs, restitution takes place. David began the restoration process, when he repented unto the Lord and asked Him for forgiveness.

Psalm 51:3-4 says;

For I acknowledge my transgressions: and my sin [is] ever before me. Against thee, thee only, have I sinned, and done [this] evil in thy sight: that thou mightest be justified when thou speakest, [and] be clear when thou judgest.

David acknowledged his errors instantly and reconciled with the Lord. This reconciliation allowed the Lord to use David further. God had a purpose for David, and that purpose had to be accomplished. The young man referred to earlier was released from jail after three years.

Later he embarked on putting his life together. He started to see wisdom ascribed to the correction process. He turned his ways around and started to fellowship with the right group of friends; those who are godly and following God's purposes for their lives. Here are examples of what happens when correction is achieved. This is not all encompassing, just to give you an idea:

In the process of correction,

- The gambler would normally leave the chips behind; he will stop squandering his God-given money.
- The drug dealer would hang up the guns and drug use; there will be no need to contaminate the body with foreign substance; then kill someone else for not cooperating with you on a failed drug deal.
- The smoker would leave the cigarettes behind; and would know that his body is the temple of the Holy Spirit; the body does not need to inhale what could cause lung cancer and other deadly diseases.
- The drinker would abandon the bottle; knowing that being drunk causes all kinds of harm; for instance, damage to his kidney and urinary system. Unfortunately, accidents and many more ills are caused by that.
- The families would reconcile because of correction.

In politics, this same phenomenon works. President Barack Obama started his presidency in January 2009. In November of 2010, his party in congress was handed a severe setback and most democrats were defeated in the mid-term election. The president and his party's leaders had to make a mid-course correction, which was meant to slow down spending and create constructive ways to deal with the Republicans.

From all indications, it appears the mid-course correction is working just fine. Therefore, the PGE Fulfillment model has been designed to help you stay on course with God's purpose for your life. At times it is difficult to see or know what this purpose is, but that's why you have people of intellect who are filled with the Holy Ghost to guide you toward your God-given purpose. A wrong turn could delay you in reaching the destiny God has planned for you.

A delayed destiny does not mean a denied destiny. It will only take you longer to achieve all God intended you to be. As you follow the leading of the Spirit, you'll find yourself excelling in the other areas that would be discussed in this book. Remember that once you achieve that focus, you can determine the best way to maximize your income and minimize your debts by the grace of God.

Chapter 1 Review

1. The ability to recognize the voice of the Holy Spirit for direction will lead you into profitable ventures and prevent you from toiling in life (Proverbs 3:5-6).

2. When you are in a difficult position, God will make a way out of the dilemma and also channel a new course for you to become successful if you trust Him (1 Corinthians 10:13).

3. Taking wrong turns in life by poor choices could lead to a bleeding financial account and eventually a wasted life (Deuteronomy 30:19).

4. A delayed destiny does not mean a denied destiny, because if you align with God's program, it will only take you longer to achieve all He intended for you (Jeremiah 29:11).

5. The failure to follow God's guidance might lead to prolonged obstacles and suffering (Matthew 11:28-30).

(2)

Maximization
Of
Income

Because the LORD thy God shall bless thee in all thine increase, and in all the works of thine hands, therefore thou shalt surely rejoice.

(Deuteronomy 16:15)

In this Chapter, you will learn about:

➢ Full Employment

➢ Proprietorship & Entrepreneurship

➢ Venture Capitalist

➢ Prudent Investing

➢ Deficit Financing

In everything you venture into, it is imperative you do the best. The best way to tackle any situation is by approaching it with your best potential. A potential is your ability to know what you can do and do well. In this chapter, I will discuss the ways in which you can maximize your income.

While you are maximizing your income, it is important that you minimize your expenses. The federal government of the United States of America tends to maximize income and maximize expenses. That's why the conservative elements of the governmental system cringe whenever they hear the word "spending."

In 2011, the Republican controlled congress in the US gave a bitter battle to the president of the United States. They claimed the president failed to control spending. In the meantime, the Republicans on their own demerit have failed to bring in income. Their Philosophy borders around giving tax breaks to the rich and wealthy. Their philosophy also is to tax the poor. This philosophy is misguided from a heavenly perspective and earthly viewpoint. A misguided policy must not be pushed down to the inhabitants of the nations.

Maximization of income is a family priority that must be taken very seriously. Without the right degree of income, a family can be broken up and apart.

As I outlined in the chapter page, full employment, proprietorship, venture capitalism, prudent investing, and deficit financing would serve as the bedrock of this chapter. My favorite of all these forms of income maximization is deficit financing.

FULL EMPLOYMENT

Full employment is defined as when a person has a job. A job is a piece of work a person attends to daily, weekly or monthly provided that they are receiving a W-2 or a Form 1099 or any other form of tax evidence of work at the end of the year to file their taxes. Full employment brings joy to the person who was hired. The process for full employment is that you apply for a job and are given it, when you fulfill the company's requirements.

On your first day of work, your new supervisor or manager will probably assign you your new role. It is your responsibility to be diligent with it. At the end of the week or month, you are compensated as agreed. Many homes suffer the challenge of full employment. A lot of relationships are endangered because spouses are busy working in different locations, not having time to be together. Another down side to full employment is that it ties you down.

When you are working full time for an organization, their agenda becomes your agenda. Their aspirations become your aspirations. You would not be able to dream big because you are busy fulfilling their dreams. You are waiting in the wings for someone else to *move on* so you can *move up*. After a while, you would find yourself stranded and strapped in one position, possibly one or two rotations on the job.

Whenever you are caged by the elements of a full employment, it becomes very hard to dream big. There are arguments to be made for the advantages of full employment; here are some pointers that seem to show the value of full employment.

(1) *Full employment brings security:* The security full employment brings, helps the worker to believe next week is taken care of. In a spiritual sense, this is a caged mentality. The true security is the one found in the Lord.

The Bible says;

He that dwells in the secret place of the Most High shall abide under the shadow of the Almighty.

(Psalm 91:1)

The Almighty God is the One who can grant whatever protection you desire. The security in full employment is as false as it is stated in Psalms 115:1-5;

Not unto us, O Lord, not unto us, but unto thy name give glory, for thy mercy, and for thy truth's sake. [2]Wherefore should the heathen say, where is now their God? [3]But our God is in the heavens: he hath done whatsoever he hath pleased. [4]Their idols are silver and gold, the work of men's hands. [5]They have mouths, but they speak not: eyes have they, but they see not.

The Lord made it absolutely clear that when you base your trust in idols (full employment). You would have lost ground with God. Many people refuse to go to church on Sunday or any church day because of their jobs. It appears to me that they would have missed the mark by relying on a career to propel them. It is the Lord that propels you.

(2) Full Employment brings joy: On the day you were hired, you were full of joy, excitement, rejoicing, and hope. Before the job came, you promised the Lord you would bless His Name with substance. However, on your first pay from work, and after you have determined what your net pay will be, God is no longer in your agenda. The reason for it is that you would have factored in your bill payment and forgotten about the works of the Lord.

The Bible says;

> *…The joy of the Lord is our strength.*
>
> (Nehemiah 8:10)

The joy from this job does not surpass the joy from the Lord. God's servant, Nehemiah was expressing the upmost joy that's received. This is usually the case when you are aligned, connected and affiliated with God. He said that this joy is no longer a mere joy; instead, it is a joy that turns into strength.

(3) ***Full employment tends to carry contentment.*** Everyone that is fully employed sees themselves as being content with what they are doing. They inevitably pursue a career with their full might and strength.

> *Finally, my brethren, be strong in the Lord, and in the power of his might.*
>
> (Ephesians 6:10)

Paul, the Apostle in admonishing the Ephesians allowed them to see that their strength is in the Lord, and that's why he told them to be "strong." To be strong means to have a great degree of contentment. The Apostle was careful to state where this strength ought to be. So he said "be strong in the Lord."

When you are completely aligned with the vision of God for your life, then and only then can you experience the power of his might. Contentment can only be achieved when the might of God is deposited in you. The might of God can also be seen as the mind of God.

No wonder Paul the Apostle in writing to the Christians in Philippi, said;

> *Let this mind be in you, which was also in Christ Jesus.*
>
> (Philippians 2:5)

Please do not be confused; I am not saying that full employment is a bad thing. What I am saying is that it serves as a good source of income, but do not let your life revolve around it. In order to have a balanced life, you must bring into perspective your job and your spiritual living. Most people have departed from their faith because of their jobs.

They regard their jobs as a source of full sufficiency. They do not attend midweek meetings and even fail to go for the regular Sunday worship meetings because of the demands on their time, created by their jobs.

The Bible is clear on the issue.

If any would not work, neither should he eat.

(2 Thessalonians 3:10)

But this book advocates a balance in career and spiritual life.

PROPRIETORSHIP VERSUS ENTREPRENEURSHIP

The United States government is very friendly towards small business enterprises. The government tends to grant them tax breaks and in addition, offers them training needed to make the business prosper. The US government also has established various avenues for small business owners to network and market their products and services.

One of such agencies is the Small Business Administration (SBA). The SBA helps small businesses that are starting up by providing all kinds of business assistance. The government also encourages small business owners to join their local chamber of commerce. In the Chamber of Commerce, the businesses network and find out what they can do for one another. The notion of proprietorship is equivalent with that of an Entrepreneurial Organization. The concepts, thoughts and mannerisms are very similar.

Due to the fact that maximizing income from a self start perspective is very important, it is critical to discuss the nature and essence of the proprietorship or the entrepreneurial organization; the leadership style of Moses when the children of Israel left Egypt; the challenges that proprietors might face, and how to keep the organization's spirit alive.

The Nature and Essence

(Mintzberg, Alhstrand, and Lampel, 1998) present 10 schools of strategy - design, planning, positioning, entrepreneurial, cognitive, learning, power, cultural, environmental, and configuration. Each of the school performs a strategic operation to ensure the success of the organization. Every facet of the business strategy points to the fact that one business owner is the glue that would hold together the organization.

It is the entrepreneurial business strategy. This type of strategy assumes much depth in business acumen; it is when an individual acts like an organization and is driven by pure passion about the vision of success and the willingness to bear significant inherent risks for the good of the organization (Mintzberg et al., 1998).

The role of the entrepreneur is greater than merely "starting a business." (Watson, 2010) notes that entrepreneurship is often a process through which a person of passion would identify opportunities, allocate resources, and create value. The creation of this value is driven by the passion of satisfying unmet needs or the identification of opportunities for change. The business owner mentally converts "problems" into "opportunities", then embarks on an action to identify the solutions to those problems and the customers who will pay to have those problems solved.

The concept and strategic purposes of an entrepreneur could be further analyzed from a variety of business perspectives, such as the nature of the business, managerial, and personal perspectives. The underlying theme of the entrepreneur centers on specific behavioral patterns, according to (Hisrich et al., 2005);

(1) The ability to take initiative,
(2) The organizing and reorganizing of social and economic mechanisms to turn resources and situations to practical account,
(3) The acceptance of risk or failure.

Translating the entrepreneurship to various disciplines, the economist sees the entrepreneur as a resource hub for labor, materials, and other assets that would create a greater value for the enterprise.

The psychologist sees the entrepreneur as "typically driven by certain forces" in order to satisfy the urge to accomplish certain psychological-business needs (Hisrich, et al., 2005).

Finally, (Hisrich et al., 2005) writes, "the businessman views the entrepreneur as a threat, an aggressive competitor, whereas to another businessman, the same entrepreneur may be an ally, a source of supply, a customer, or someone who creates wealth for others, as well as finds better ways to utilize resources, reduce waste, and produce jobs others are glad to get."

(Mintzberg, Alhstrand, and Lampel, 1998) describe the entrepreneurial school as a strategy formation for the visionary process, noting that "vision [forms] a mental representation of strategy, created or at least expressed in the head of the leader. That vision serves as both an inspiration and a sense of what needs to be done - a guiding idea..." (Page 124).

Certain characteristics define this leader; the leader searches for new opportunities to grow the organization; the leader centralizes the power of the organization in his or her hands; the leader entertains bold moves in the face of uncertainty; the leader primarily finds a way to grow the organization and makes it the focus.

Furthering the principles shared by Hisrich, Peters, and Shepherd, (Mintzberg et al., 1998) provided a contemporary summary of the premises of the entrepreneurial view of the strategic leader noting that;

1. The entrepreneur formulates the visionary sentiments as basic "perspective" with an eye for the future and making long-range decisions for the good of the organization.

2. The overall strategy process is "rooted in the experience and intuition" of the strategist or leader. Originally, some thoughts and ideas leading to this venture could be based on learned patterns and experience from other dealings.

3. When the leader decides to follow up with the venture, he or she would pursue this "vision single-mindedly" and become intimately involved in all of the necessary processes to implement the venture.

4. "The strategic vision is thus malleable, and so entrepreneurial strategy tends to be deliberate and emergent – deliberate in overall vision and emergent in how the details of the vision unfold" (Page 143).

5. The entrepreneurial organization gives much latitude to the owner in order to structure the organization in the way he or she envisioned it.

6. "The entrepreneurial strategy tends to take the form of niche, one or more pockets of market position protected from the forces of outright competition" (Page 143).

Leadership of Moses

In the era of Moses, the servant of the Lord, there was need for him to change the leadership style, so that it can be more functional. He operated as an entrepreneur. He was the man with the vision and had the ultimate strategy on where the children of Israel would be. After a discussion with Jethro, his father-in law, Moses had a refined expectation and a properly defined vision on how to be a good leader to the children of Israel. The leadership method of Moses ensured that the leaders of the twelve tribes would participate in leading the folks.

He made them accountable for their decisions. He allowed them the flexibility to dream and have vision of how to coordinate activities in each tribe. In the meantime, the overall vision remained with Moses. God used Jethro to filter the vision in order for Moses to be an effective leader in his enterprise.

Jethro explained to Moses that there would be no reason for him to adjudicate all cases big and small. He showed Moses the principles of streamlining activities.

Due to the fact that Moses received the instructions of Jethro, he became a successful leader, and the children of Israel moved forward (See Exodus 18).

Challenges for an Entrepreneur

Although an entrepreneur could experience great growth on the onset of the business in this modern business era, business owners must continually remain vigilant about certain forces that can kill or harm the existence of the entrepreneurship.

Paul Lemberg, in 2002, identified some mistakes that can harm the organization noting that many of the mistakes are sometimes unavoidable, even when the entrepreneur has an experienced hand in the business.

Victim of big customer syndrome: This is when an entrepreneur relies on a very few sources of income, for instance if one of the customers contributes approximately 50 percent of the revenues. This creates a huge vulnerability for the proprietor because if he loses that customer, the business might experience a huge set back. The proprietor must keep looking for new customers and finding ways to increase business channels. The entrepreneur should conduct local research and test a product upfront before rolling it out.

For instance, a new proprietor that moves into a food court in a major mall would have to give free samples to patrons as they walk pass his restaurants. When the patrons like the sample tasted, they might walk in to patronize the eatery.

Low-price leader: Some entrepreneurs embark on their venture with the mindset that they would serve as the low-price player in their market and make profits on the volume. This strategy has not been very successful; therefore, a new enterprise must ensure that the cost related to a service or product is properly covered.

Short on capital: Many small business owners tend to start with too-optimistic sales projections, too-short product development timeframes, and too low expense forecasts. No matter the reason for this type of projection, the business must avoid the temptation of being undercapitalized. The business owner must anticipate an economic downturn and maintain some reserves; all projections must have the elements of conservatism and reserve enough capital for the next planned round of funding.

Ideas need to be in-focus: The original idea should not be discounted for many ideas clouding the judgment of the entrepreneur. Instead of focusing on the core product, service, market, distribution channel the business owner starts to dabble in areas outside the original vision; thereby, spreading thin the meager resource that the organization has, and performing at a mediocre level.

Product's return on investment: The entrepreneur must perform analysis that articulate return on investment for the customer to justify their investment in the organization. An impressive return would mean a repeat experience by the customer. To achieve this, the business owner must establish a relationship with the customer by meeting or exceeding their needs and expectations.

Admit mistakes: The entrepreneur must admit errors or mistakes and redress them immediately. There is no need engaging in a shouting match with the customer. Learn from the mistakes and move on.

Adding to Peter Lemberg's challenges for entrepreneurs, Robin Low in 2010 provided a list of items considered top challenges facing small businesses and entrepreneurs:

Talent: The entrepreneur runs into the challenge of finding and retaining qualified workers in his organization. Most talented employees are concerned about the viability of the enterprise, as such, they may choose to enlist with a more established and profit making organization.

Marketing and public relations: Due to the fact that the knowledge and brain thrust of the business rest on the business owner, and if the owner does not have good marketing knowledge or background, more than likely, the marketing and public relations of the enterprise might suffer. Therefore, the entrepreneur must quickly learn creative marketing, and targeting public relations to spread awareness of his product and services.

Brand equity: Brand equity is essential for a business growth. Without a good product brand, the small business might face tough challenges to stay alive. As a new business, the entrepreneur must enlist the help of reputable firms to introduce the product or service to the public.

Cash-flow: The entrepreneur must see the role of cash-flow as pivotal to the success of the business. He should ensure that no mismanaged cash-flow exists in the business and all the control points are instituted for the viability of the enterprise.

State and federal regulations: One key area of challenge for the entrepreneur involves governmental regulations and compliance provisions. New enterprises that do not use adequate counseling system might get in trouble with the regulatory agencies, and at worst be fined or shut down for lack of compliance.

Equally important is knowing the governmental agencies responsible for granting loans and grants to help with the financial position of the entrepreneurial organization.

Economic uncertainty: During difficult economic times, it is hard to start a business due to the nature of uncertainty. The economic mood does not encourage starting a new enterprise, instead the entrepreneur enters the arena with less than full confidence. The economic condition normally would affect the business budget and the participation of the consumers in patronizing the new venture.

Keeping up with technology: Another challenge for the entrepreneur is the advancement in technology. Since the mid-90's, technology has progressed very fast. The business entrepreneur would have to make a concerted effort to keep up with the tech era. The enterprise stands to gain from using the latest and greatest technology tools, and from ordering to tracking inventory to compiling customer data to improve business flow.

Access to capital: The entrepreneur needs to have good access to capital for the business to grow. The business enterprise needs working capital to run operationally, and needs capital to purchase big-ticket items that would help in the production cycle of the business.

Undercapitalization may inhibit the growth and sometimes would cause a company to fail, as such, it is important for the entrepreneur to maintain meaningful contacts and relationships to help the business in time of need.

Igniting and Keeping the Vision Alive

Having seen the challenges that the entrepreneur faces and how complex these challenges are, it is important for the light in the vision to remain unquenched.

The fire shall ever be burning upon the altar; it shall never go out.

(Leviticus 6:13)

An entrepreneur who allows his vision to die because of a few challenges here and there would have failed to actualize their dream. The story of 3M is very compelling and motivating in promoting entrepreneurial spirit. The success of 3M catapulted it to 51st place on the Fortune's list of top companies (Lehr, 1980). As an organization with many sides, 3M believes its success results from its entrepreneurial spirit in the organization despite its size.

(Leher, 1980) writes of 3M, "We keep these stories alive and often repeat them so that any employee with an entrepreneurial spirit who feels discouraged, frustrated, and ineffective in a large organization knows that he or she is not the first one to face considerable odds" (Page 31). Debbie Gisonni, a world-class entrepreneur, shares ten ways to accomplish a vision, noting that the entrepreneur is constantly looking for ways to improve business conditions and constantly, seeking and implementing changes that would strengthen the vision.

Stay in touch with former colleagues: An entrepreneur must continually stay in touch with former colleagues and be abreast with the latest information. This network of information could serve as good leverage to boost the spirit of the new organization. The entrepreneur must not suffer "I am not part of that world anymore" syndrome anymore. The entrepreneur must retain a mailing list and keep old colleagues informed about the progress of the organization.

Network! Network!! Network!!!: Keep a meaningful relationship with friends and family members that can provide a much needed help to a start-up organization. Friends and family members can provide assistance in the area of staffing, finances, and marketing. This network could also help with bringing much needed customers by promoting the products and services of the entrepreneurial organization.

***Propose "win-win" partnerships with corporate America*:** The entrepreneur must develop meaningful relationships that can enhance the cause of the vision. Institute the use of the theory in sales called the "funnel concept" by making connections, phone calls, and meetings. The concept shows the trickling out the bottom in the way of sales.

***Drop the "I can't" Attitude*:** The entrepreneur cannot be caught making excuses of how impossible the tasks have become. The entrepreneur should remain firm and steadfast, and in the process earn the respect and attain the response needed from people inside and outside the organization.

***Act like a real company*:** The entrepreneur must allow his organization to act like a functioning enterprise. Although the organization might not be flourishing in millions of dollars, the attitude and disposition must be professional and focused. The days of commingling personal and business funds should come to an automatic end. Therefore, business disciplines must be taken seriously! The organization should produce a Profit and Loss Statement and a Balance Sheet to access the viability of the enterprise. As a new venture, the eyes of the proprietor should be set on ensuring that the organization makes money and not lose money.

Publicity: There needs to be a greater advocate for developing a relationship with the local media; this media relationship would bring about the exposure and publicity the entrepreneur needs. Residents in community should know about the business and what it does. Freely grant interviews to the local newspaper and press to ensure name recognition. Consider signing up some local volunteers and grant internships to local college students.

Create events: Encourage staff to become creative with ideas that would create visibility for the organization. Visit the local chamber of commerce and understand the common business needs of the community. Consider these needs; sponsor events that would be beneficial to the residents. Understand existing community programs and participate in them. Support the activities and events of local churches and schools.

Save Money: The entrepreneur must find ways to conserve cost and save money, not just trying to raise money. Saving money encourages the agenda of an entrepreneurial spirit. The organization has to find better ways of doing things such as emailing its customers instead of using regular postage.

Spread the Spirit: According to (Gisonni, 2002), "the entrepreneurial spirit is an infectious one; if you have it, others in your organization will, too" (Page 25).

The entrepreneurial spirit encourages the best in organization. People respond to such positive spirit and disposition.

According to (Gisonni, 2002), "the way to create an environment that breeds good entrepreneurs is just a matter of having good management skills; that means motivating people to stay positive, bringing them in the loop on ideas, and asking for their advice and opinions" (Page 25). The organization must be willing to share responsibility with employees and empower them to think beyond bounds. The organization should also encourage the employees to be real stakeholders with ideas and concepts and a mindset to succeed.

There are secrets that empower the organization to become successful in their endeavors. These secrets are embodied in a leadership article published by the Knowledge Center of Wharton School of Business. The secrets note that in order to be an entrepreneurial leader, you must do the following, (Gisonni 2002) writes:

"First, take responsibility for the uncertain outcome of new projects. You must be able to say to employees, "If I'm wrong, it's my problem, not yours." This allows employees to operate under uncertainty without worrying about the repercussions should the project fail.

Secondly, outline the challenges that push employees to their limits. But know when a challenge may push workers beyond their abilities. Thirdly, get support from the key stakeholders inside and outside your organization. To operate as an entrepreneurial manager, you'll need to convince decision-makers to back you up when things go wrong or right. Fourthly, build commitment from employees. You must foster a willingness among employees to work toward a common goal. You need to motivate and cultivate effective teams. Lastly, make the most of people resources.

Break down team members' perceptions and stereotypes of what can and can't be done. You'll need a sense of how people resources have been undervalued".

Adapted from knowledge@Wharton

VENTURE CAPITALISM

This chapter deals with the concept of maximizing income. In every aspect of your life, there has to be an area or a room for risk taking. Most successful people we know today have taken one degree of risk or another. Playing it safe is not the way to go. In the story of the talents in the Bible, the steward who hid his talent because he was being cautious was not rewarded. He was called "wicked" (See Matthew 25).

George Soros, the famed billionaire, gained his fortune by engaging in risky ventures. When you become overly cautious, there is a tendency to make a mistake; thus, countering your original objective of being cautious. In venture capitalism, you are encouraged to take risks. The risk must be measured and calculated.

It also should be sound and rewarding. The reason why a venture capitalist fails is because they did not surround themselves with elements of risk mitigation. The risk mitigation process deals with cautionary activities that relate to you taking the risk. Therefore, a failure to follow such caution can create dire consequences.

Let me share with you some venture capitalism principles:

(1) *The venture capitalist takes risks*: This risk process normally would have some awesome rewards in the end. As a venture capitalist, you end up dealing with other people and finding out their interests. You make a decision whether or not to fund a project.

A case in point: In 2005, I received a telephone call to fund a particular project. I pulled out $55,000 from my 401(k) to fund this project. Seven months into the deal, the wheels came off and I lost all of the money.

It became clear to me that I needed to seek the face of God before attempting a venture of that magnitude. My failure to seek God's guidance resulted in such a huge loss. Please note that I am not saying that I was duped, but that the protective hands of God were not on the project. The gentleman that who took the money is still alive and well. The morale of this story is that every undertaking is a venture that must be presented before the Lord.

(2) *The rewards of venture capitalism could be great:* When you receive an approval from the God regarding a particular deal, there are chances that you can make up for all other losses.

The Bible says;

For I know the thoughts that I think toward you, saith the Lord, thoughts of peace, and not of evil, to give you an expected end.
(Jeremiah 29:11)

Since the plans God has for you are awesome, delightful, and glorious, therefore, there should be no shaking, no toiling, and no fretting in the ventures you are a part of. In Acts 27, the Bible records that Apostle Paul was being sailed to Rome and on his way, there arose a tempestuous wind, called Euroclydon. While everyone on the ship was fretful and afraid, Paul stood on solid ground.

He announced to them on the ship that the angel of the Lord, whose he is, and whom he served, visited with him at night and said, *"be of good cheer"* (Acts 27:25). Because Paul was on that ship, it did not matter whether Euroclydon was in the second degree or not, they were going to make it to shore. So, it is with you and your venture capital; because you are a part of the deal, your funding cannot go down the drain. Just as Paul and the 276 people made it safely to shore, so also you will make it to shore.

(3) *Venture capitalism encourages creativity*: The creative juices will run high in the mind of the venture capitalist. The venture capitalist finds ways to formulate a deal. The capitalist will come up with ideas that are not traditional. These ideas will yield maximum income for the capitalist and maximum joy for the recipient. During the deal process, it would appear that the capitalist might lose some money but as the deal matures, the capitalist ends up smiling all the way to the bank.

The Bible says in Proverbs 4:18;

But the path of the just is as the shining light, that shines more and more unto the perfect day.

So, the path of the capitalist shines forever. And the shining path creates maximum income.

PRUDENT INVESTING

Life has shown that there are winning ways to becoming prudent. Over the years I have learned and seen those people investing prudently end up making good money. A prudent investor is one who undertakes the necessary investigative research in order to determine if a particular investment venture is safe and practical.

For instance, in the stock market, a prudent investor would research the stock of interest before investing in it. The research performed by the investor helps with making a "go" or "no go" decision.

Below are some key principles surrounding Prudent Investing:

(1) *Investing in a 401(K) plan*: This principle is really a type of investment. A worker is encouraged to invest a percentage of his earnings on a monthly basis. At the same time, the company would match a percentage of what the worker invested. This is a great way to save money fast. Assuming the portfolio in which this amount is saved becomes very successful, the prudent investor would have made a wise decision. Another advantage in participating in a 401(K) savings plan is that taxes are deferred.

The deferred taxes serve as a basis for reduced income exposed to current taxation. As such, the investor has made a very good call.

(2) ***The prudent investor would build meaningful relationships:*** This would happen when the investor seeks to understand various investment portfolio plans. The investor would discuss his or her options with various investment portfolio managers to understand the consequences of the options presented by the portfolio manager. This in effect broadens the relationship network of the investors.

(3) ***Investing in real estate:*** The prudent investor is one who invests in real estate ventures within their state or outside his state. It has been determined that real estate investment serves as a very good and viable investment option. Please note that in the recent years, the value of real estate investment has declined because of the housing bubble.

The government found that there were many financial institutions granting real estate loans to individuals who could not afford them. This created a high default rate and as such, a resounding foreclosure epidemic. Today, it appears that real estate investment is no longer attractive, but that's not true. Like anything else, the real estate market hit a snag that it would recover from.

(4) ***Prudent investing in insurance deals***: Several insurance companies, such as New York Life, offer a product whereby the cash surrender value of a life insurance policy can be redeemed over a period of time. The way this works is that a policy holder is asked to pay an annual fee for which a policy is designed for their specific need. After the annual fee is paid, year after year, there is a maturity value assigned to the policy from which cash can be redeemed.

It is possible that there are other products within the insurance industry that are similar to this discussed, however this serves as an example for what could be achieved using an insurance policy. Therefore, a prudent investor opens up their antenna to see various forms of investing. This insurance policy could particularly be beneficial for a family interested in sending their children to college.

DEFICIT FINANCING

This is my favorite of all of the options. The reason for it is that decisions are based on the fact that the nuts and bolts of deficit financing are covered in the scripture. This type of financing desires a lot of faith.

In line with this, the Bible states;

Now there cried a certain woman of the wives of the sons of the prophets unto Elisha, saying, Thy servant my husband is dead; and thou knowest that thy servant did fear the Lord: and the creditor is come to take unto him my two sons to be bondmen. [2]And Elisha said unto her, what shall I do for thee? Tell me, what hast thou in the house? And she said, Thine handmaid hath not any thing in the house, save a pot of oil. [3]Then he said, Go, borrow thee vessels abroad of all thy neighbors, even empty vessels; borrow not a few. [4]And when thou are come in, thou shalt shut the door upon the and upon thy sons, and shalt pour out into all those vessels, and thou shalt set aside that which is full. [5]So she went from him, and shut the door upon her and upon her sons, who brought the vessels to her; and she poured out. [6]And it came to pass, when the vessels were full, that she said unto her son, Bring me yet a vessel. And he said unto her, there is not a vessel more. And the oil stayed. [7]The she came and told the man of God. And he said, Go, sell the oil, and pay thy debt, and live thou and they children of the rest.

(2 Kings 4:1-7)

Let us discuss the principles:

(1) *Totally broke equals back against the wall*: The story from 2 Kings shows that the lady in focus was totally broke. This lady had lost her husband who was a prophet. During the prophet's active ministry, the woman who was highly in debt sought for his help, because of the harassment of her creditor.

She expressed her fear, discontentment, and disappointment to the man of God. She had no money. Her back was against the wall. She had no job, no food stamps, and had lost hope. She became so afraid. She faced a period of toiling. She was shaken. She was weary. She had lost it all. In today's parallelism, her home was facing foreclosure. As a tenant, she was facing eviction.

Her car was being repossessed and the man in charge of the repossession was always knocking at her door. Her credit cards had been cancelled because they had been maxed-out and there had been no payments made. Her back was truly against the wall. Then, she boldly approached the man of God.

(2) *Deficit financer must have faith*: In the creative scheme of deficit financing, the individual who has been terrorized by the enemy needs to have faith and not fear.

The Bible says;

"Because she had lost all, her kids were being required as collateral"
                                    (2 Kings 4: 1b, Paraphrased).

Whenever kids are being used as collateral, the situation has to be really bad. The gravity of the matter gave her enough faith to approach the prophet.

In Paul's Epistle to the Romans;

For therein is the righteousness of God revealed from faith to faith: as it is written, the just shall live by faith.

(Romans 1:17)

It is clear that this woman had lived in fear for a long time, especially after her husband died. The principles of faith were not on her side at all but by the time she had to use her children as collateral, faith kicked in.

(3) *There must be a relationship with people*: When the woman was undergoing her difficulties, it appears that every neighbor, friend, family, and foes knew of her problems, but could not do anything about it. And so, when Prophet Elisha asked the woman to bring forth some containers, she was able to go ask her neighbors, family, friends, and foes for such. A relationship is something built over time. It is something that allows someone else to trust another. Relationships are always needed in the day of adversity. When Prophet Elisha asked the lady to get some containers, he knew she only had limited number of containers at home. So he encouraged her to "borrow."

(4) *"Borrowing" is the meat of deficit financing*: The Bible teaches that we should owe no man and we should be no debtor to anybody while seeking prosperous adventures. The story in 2 Kings 4 gives us a bird's eye view of the mind of the Holy Spirit regarding deficit financing. In this case, the Holy Spirit proceeds to make an exception here – wherein certain circumstances could yield an immunity to borrow.

Because she aligned herself by faith to establish a relationship with the prophet, the prophet then issued an instruction that cannot be broken. The prophet said, "borrow" from folks. In the principle above, I noted that a relationship had been established and so it was easy for her to go borrow some containers from her neighbors.

(5) *Be willing to follow strange instructions*: In deficit financing, the Lord can give some strange instructions. The same God who said we should owe no man and that we are lenders and not borrowers, in this particular context provides an opportunity for this lady to get out of her mess. Why is this? Her back was truly against the wall.

Hebrews 4:16 says;

Let us therefore come boldly unto the throne of grace, that we may obtain mercy, and find grace to help in time of need.

The lady *boldly* approached the throne of grace in front of the man of God. By the aunction Of the Holy Spirit, Elisha pronounced strange utterance such as "go borrow". Whenever a man or a woman of God utters certain strange instructions, it is important to trust the anointing of God upon his or her life. If not, there will be a conflict in your mind. The strange instruction should be followed to the "Tee", because certain strange instructions are bound to test your faith. And as such, faith must be released.

The willingness of this lady to follow such strange (divine instructions) helped to accelerate her breakthrough. We have learned that obedience is better that sacrifice (1 Samuel 15:22). And in this case, the lady obeyed.

(6) *Execute on the instructions*: The instructions that were given to the lady were rather simple. The first thing the man of God asked was what she had at home. She confessed that she had nothing but a bottle of oil. This is similar to the story of 1 Kings 17, when Elijah asked the widow of Zarephath what she had at home and she proclaimed she only had bread for herself and her son to eat and die.

In that story, Elijah blessed the widow after the food was given to him and there was abundance in the home afterward.

The Prophet Elisha asked the lady to bring a bottle of oil. He also asked her to borrow some containers in addition to the ones in her possession. She did. When she came back to the prophet with the items requested for, the prophet asked that the oil be poured into the containers.

As a result, she had a tremendous financial breakthrough. Carrying out the instruction of a man of God would normally yield bountiful testimonies. The reason this woman's calamity turned into a testimony was because she faithfully heeded the instructions of the prophet.

A faithful heart is always rewarded. A careful examination of the verse of scripture shows that when the lady followed the instructions of Elisha, a particular grace was released. The grace of replenishment took effect instantly. All the containers were filled to the brim.

The containers became a source of money making mechanism for the lady. She sold the oil at the instruction of the man of God. After selling the oil, she paid off her debts and had much more left in her home. This again parallels to the widow of Zarephath who followed the instructions of Prophet Elijah, thereby invoking the grace of replenishment in her life-threatening situation. With the lady and Prophet Elisha, it was a bottle of oil. The prophet had instructed her to bring the bottle of oil and oil turned out to be lots of money.

Your situation might be different. The key to get out of any financial upheaval is to align with divine instructions. I urge you to follow these instructions for a successful deficit financing plan:

- When the money is received, you must do what you have covenanted to do. You must follow what you told the Lord that you would do.
- You must not change approach and strategies on the Lord.
- You must be a good project manager for God. Your words must be your bond.
- You must not lean on your own understanding.
- You must avoid careless schemes that will bankrupt you.
- You must continue to walk in faith and not by sight until the assignment is done.
- You must not bring in anybody that was not originally a part of the program.
- You must not present your children as collateral or mortgage their future for your own selfish desires.
- You must abstain from ungodly practices.
- You must seek the mind of God in order to receive divine instructions.
- You must be cognizant of the fact that because your back is against the wall, it does not mean you cannot leave the wall.

Chapter 2 Review

1. When you work on a full time basis for an organization, their agenda becomes yours. As a result, your progress depends solely on their advancement, but that should not be the case because our hope should be in God (Hebrews 12:2).

2. Do not despise the divine ability in you, but rather activate it and keep the fire ever burning, because the world is waiting for your manifestation (Leviticus 6:13, Romans 8:19).

3. You can only garner a huge financial fortune when you engage in calculated risky ventures. Remember, he who waits for all conditions to be favorable might not be able to take steps for a big break (Ecclesiastes 11:4).

4. I have learned and seen people investing prudently end up making good money. Therefore, it is imperative to do a comprehensive research in order to determine if a particular investment venture is safe and practical, before you embark on it (Luke 14:28).

5. The same God who said that we are lenders and not borrowers, instructed the widow in 2 Kings 4 through Prophet Elisha to borrow many vessels in order to get out of her financial despair. The key to deliverance from any financial upheaval is to align with divine instructions (2 Kings 4:3).

(3)

Budgeting

For which of you, intending to build a tower, does not sit down first and count the cost, whether he may have enough to finish it; lest perhaps, after he has laid the foundation and is not able to finish, all those seeing begin to mock him, saying, This man began to build and was not able to finish.

(Luke 14:28-30)

In this Chapter, you will learn about:

➢ Principles of Budget

➢ Types of Budget

➢ Elements of a Budget

➢ Examples of a Budget

➢ Governmental Budget

➢ Biblical Values

The major challenge with many people lies in their habitual inability to exert self-discipline in handling their finances. God did not create anyone to be a mediocre. In fact, He has greatness in store for everyone, but is left for us to attain it. The ideas you will come across in this chapter will enable you to rise above any financial challenge. Budgeting after the recession is an essential or integral part of your life.

The recession set you back. In post-recession, you move forward. In order to appropriately move forward, you have to apply the principles of budgeting in your life. Budgeting is an art, and it could also be argued to be a science. It is an art because you are compelled to perform it. It's a science because of its precision.

In this chapter, I will shed some light on the principles surrounding a good budget, also discuss the types of budget; the elements of a budget, example of a budget, and briefly look at a governmental budget, and biblical values for a budget.

PRINCIPLES OF BUDGETS

(1) *Management Tool to Measure Performance*: It is a management tool that tends to evaluate the performance of a business.

As a management tool, a budget looks at how budget managers perform. Each manager is held accountable for the resulting outcome of the budget. The resulting outcome of the budget defines the next level for that manager. The manager is either promoted for a good budget handling, or penalized for mishandling the budget.

My prayer for you is that the demon of mismanagement will be destroyed in your life in the Name of Jesus, Amen!

For promotion [cometh] neither from the east, nor from the west, nor from the south.

(Psalms 75:6)

The Bible notes that God has the ability to promote and demote, based on your works and your heart towards Him.

You can easily assume that God rewards those who manage their affairs wisely, and punishes those who mismanage theirs. In the story of the talents, we find that the man with one talent failed to manage properly and so his talent was taken from him and given to someone else who was able to manage the affairs of his master (Matthew 25:14-30).

(2) *Provides Guidance:* As a management tool (and people tool), a budget serves as guidance. The budget is the roadmap for every financial success. A man without a road map normally does not do well. A roadmap is an impetus for success. It creates direction, and provides navigation. It guides in times of difficulties. As the recession has come to an end, budgeting becomes the key player in your financial situation. It tells you when to spend and when not to spend. It advises you to curtail unnecessary expenses.

A person with a philanthropic mind is often tempted to overspend because those in need of help are always pulling on him or her. Without this guiding tool, the philanthropist might be stuck in recession whereas others are prospering. Whenever there is a doubt in your financial circumstances, please endeavor to recheck your roadmap.

(3) *Budget Stresses Accountability:* A society where no one is accountable is a society with chaos. A budget stresses accountability because someone needs to be held responsible for how money is being spent. In a family, there needs to be discussion between the man and woman as to who should be responsible for the family budget. In most cases, when this decision is made, and if the budget succeeds, the budget owner is praised and rewarded with a family dinner or extra shopping money.

On the other hand, if the budget fails, the responsible party gets the blame and the family ends up with unnecessary strife. As we all know, money is an area the enemy uses to attack the family. As such, prudence needs to be exercised in order for families to stay in harmony and remain together. Let us say for example, in the Jones family, Mrs. Jones became the budget manager as agreed upon by Mr. & Mrs. Jones.

When the budget failed, Mrs. Jones performed an audit of the budget, and she found that Mr. Jones had been breaching the terms of family money spending. Mrs. Jones took offense to the breach and after several breaches, decided that a divorce was now necessary. There are several horrible stories about budget breaches in families which end up creating relationship havoc. Being a pastor, it is important for me to state that your families must be careful in the dispensation of budgeting duties and assignments.

(4) *Control Mechanism:* As a mechanism, the budget becomes a tool that institutes discipline in people's lives. Whenever there is a control mechanism, we are really talking about allowing things to follow proper order. As a control point, the budget master must adhere to the standards of the budget. The budget master must not sway to the left or to the right. He must remain focused, disciplined, and directed.

As a controlling tool, a budget becomes a mechanism for instituting error detection in the implementation process. Large variances in actual dollars versus budget dollars indicate a basis for good research.

(5) *Realistic Projections:* In the budgeting process, the budget master must learn to be candid in his projection. In a lot of cases, the budget master loses sight of the main picture, by making unrealistic projections. This unrealistic projection normally brings the budget to its knees. The fall of the budget creates financial chaos. In the period of recession, you cannot operate in financial chaos. That's why it is important for you to follow the designed plans for your home and your small business.

(6) *Discourage Irresponsibility:* Because the budget is such an integral part of success, it is important that budget handlers are responsible in their thoughts, words and deeds. As a result of that, they cannot pass on irresponsible budgeting techniques. Whoever is handling the budget for your homes must have a record of consistent responsibility.

This is a role that must be discharged with credibility and integrity. The character of the budget handler is important here.

...but let your yea be yea; and your nay, nay; lest ye fall into condemnation.

(James 5:12)

This particular viewpoint in the budget process would help the family get to the next level. Please, an irresponsible budget manager should not be allowed to manage the budget. This is important because he or she will ruin the family finances.

TYPES OF BUDGET

In order to have an effective budget, the budget master must be cognizant of timing. A budget must have a particular time period. A timeless budget is a nonsense budget. But when the budget is designed with a time period, everyone who is subject to that budget will work within the timeframe allocated to it. This is important because when the budget period ends, there is always a need to evaluate the performance of everyone responsible. Let us discuss some budget periods.

(1) *Yearly Budget:* This is a budget that covers the entire year, it covers the 12 months from January to December. The budget must be reasonable because it is covering the entire year, and because of this, it is important that this budget is carefully followed.

In this budget, there is need for the key players to speak their minds and share with the budget manager events and activities they know will occur during the year.

For example, assuming a family plans to go on a vacation trip at the end of July, the budget manager would need to account for that in the budget. Also, if the family plans to pay back some taxes, they should account for that in their budgets when taxes are due. A failure to have critical events included in the budget would create unnecessary spikes and variances in the budget.

Also, a failure to properly plan vacation and other known events could create a room for criticizing the budget manager. Overall, including known events during the budget process helps the budget to be more real and manageable.

(2) *Semi-Annual Budget:* This type of budget is similar to the annual budget, except that it only covers a six month period. The characteristics described in the annual budget also apply here. This six month budget is easily manageable because the budget manager only has a window of six months to make adjustments, correct the course, and finalize another six month budget.

(3) *Quarterly Budget:* The quarterly budget can also assume the characteristics of the semi-annual budget. The quarterly budget represents three months only. It is very hard for the budget master to be off the tangent in this type of budget. The budget master is only dealing with three months at a time. The advantage of the quarterly budget is that the budget master would have the opportunity to compare quarter by quarter; and decisions can then be made whether another quarter should be adjusted or corrected based on the quarter to quarter information.

(4) *Monthly Budget:* This is the most common form of budgeting. It is derived from the annual budget. Note that when the annual budget is designed and adopted, the budget master breaks the annual budget into 12 periods. The monthly budget considers 30-31 days of operation. It is very effective because during the month, the budget master can identify abuses.

This type of budget serves as a great tool for comparing against actual. The monthly budget serves as the background for all kinds of projections and forecasts. In a family, the monthly budget is the basis for management.

ELEMENTS OF A BUDGET

Due to the fact that budgeting is such an important part of a family's financial growth, it is imperative to know the elements that make up the budget.

(1) *Inflow:* This represents the sources of funds. Your money could come from your employment, business, gifts, loans, and so on. This is the basis for the budget. For instance, if the budget master plans to collect a total of $100,000 for an annual period, that is what he will include in the budget.

(2) *Outflow:* This is the spending arm of the budget. The budget master gets a lot of heat about this. The budget master lists out different expenses that make up the outflow. By definition, outflow is the money that would be spent during the budget period. It is a simple concept, but one that is hard to follow.

In the example above, the budget master has several major categories to manage, including tithes, housing, family, transportation, utilities and credit cards. The danger here is that there might be items not accounted for. Normally those expenses would create a huge variance in the budget. Therefore, the budget manager and others responsible for designing the budget should ensure a comprehensive budget is submitted.

(3) Bottom Line: This concept is easily defined as the excess of inflow over outflow; unless there is a deficit in which outflow exceeds inflow. Everyone is supposed to support the budget in a way that the bottom line is positive. The federal government of the United States always struggles to determine the bottom line number.

Owing to the fact that President Obama's administration constantly contends with the Republican congress to ensure that more monies are collected from the rich in form of taxes. The Republicans have a mandate to constantly reduce the taxes for the wealthy. As a result of this misguided thought, it is hard for the administration to balance the budget.

(4) Variances: This is the difference between budget and actual. The variance is positive when the actual inflows are greater than the budgeted inflows. That means if the budget inflow is $100,000 and the actual money collected is $120,000; then there is a positive variance in the budget.

In the case of expenses, if the budgeted dollars for spending or outflows exceed the actual dollars spent, that would yield a positive variance; however, if the actual spending is greater than the budgeted spending, then there is negative variance. Whenever there is a negative variance, the budget master tries hard to explain the reason behind it.

As discussed in the principles of budgeting above, it is important to note that the budget column entitled "variance" is the basis for which performance is evaluated. A poor variance could get someone fired and a good variance could earn someone a promotion.

EXAMPLE OF A BUDGET

The following is an example of a budget for the Smith family. It reflects that the Smith family received wages of about $55,000 from full-time employment, $35,000 from their business, and $10,000 from interest earned from Deficit financing. The total income is $100,000. This is good income after surviving a brutal recession. The Smith family must not get complacent and say this is enough income; if there are additional opportunities for them to bring in more money, they must aspire accordingly.

My position in terms of aspiring for more money is that you do not allow the chase for it derail you from the will of God. Instead of pursuing money with all your heart and soul, you should keep the words of Matthew 6:33 engraved in your palm and heart:

But seek ye first the kingdom of God, and his righteousness; and all these things shall be added unto you.

In this example, the Smith family paid 10% in tithes. In this budget, the Smith family ended up spending a total of $81,000 for the year and they ended up with $19,000.

Please see the table below:

Budget for the Smith Family		
For the Year 2011		
Sources of INFLOWS		
Income from Wages	$ 55,000.00	55%
Income from Business	35,000.00	35%
Income from Interest	10, 000.00	10%
Total Income/INFLOWS	$ 100,000.00	100%
Sources of OUTFLOWS		
Tithes	$ 10,000.00	12%
Housing	18, 000.00	22%
Food	5, 000.00	6%
Utilities	12, 000.00	15%
Transportation	6,000.00	7%
Credit Cards	15, 000.00	19%
Other	15, 000.00	19%
Total Expenses/OUTFLOWS	$ 81,000.00	100%
Bottom Line	$ 19, 000.00	

You can use the above tabular presentation for your budgeting template. It is important that you use the expenses that relate to you.

For instance, you may not have an expense line called "Credit Cards", as such; you should not have it in your list of expenses. In the meantime, the chart below represents a graphical presentation of the expenses. Based on this chart, the Smith family can now determine which expenses to trim.

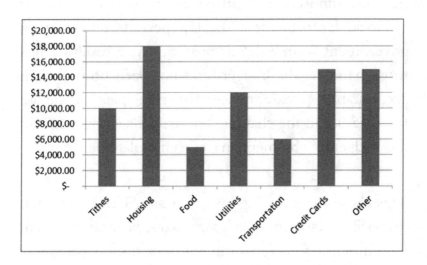

GOVERNMENTAL BUDGET

Very briefly, I would like to share with you how the federal government puts together its own budget. Lately in the news, you would have heard some wrangling between the United States political leaders about the direction of the budget. This is how the federal budget is set.

The President puts forth a vision of things to do. Then the Congress creates dollars around the vision, but due to political disagreements, the President's vision undergoes a series of negotiations with the Congress until there is an agreement on both sides. The mandate should focus on increasing inflows and decreasing outflows.

But the mindsets on both sides appear to be that of gridlock. Unfortunately, the law permits financing the government from a deficit position. As a result of this, those handling the budget have not been properly held accountable. (Please review the principles of budget listed earlier in the chapter. You would see that some of the budgetary comments have been violated).

This cause for revisiting budget basics. The government primarily gets its monies from taxes, licenses, fees, and investments. If the government does not collect any of these, we are bound to remain in a deficit for awhile.

BIBLICAL VALUES

In certain ways, the Word of God discusses elements of the budget. The Bible gives specific examples of how God used some people to carry out His divine activities.

1) Firstly, let us take a look at King Solomon.

And Solomon gave **Hiram** *twenty thousand measures of wheat for food to his household, and twenty measures of pure oil: thus gave Solomon to* **Hiram** *year by year.* [12]*And the LORD gave Solomon wisdom, as he promised him: and there was peace between* **Hiram** *and Solomon; and they two made a league together.*

(1 Kings 5:11-12)

This scripture notes that the Lord gave a mandate to King Solomon to build the temple. It is important to note that God gave him specific details to follow. Budgets work in a similar way; working with specifics and meeting the targets. Let me note that the Lord ensured that Hiram and Solomon were at peace with each other.

The expertise of Hiram became a strong basis for the building of the temple, which means that the budget manager needs to bring an expertise to the budget dialogue. The following is a list of activities that Solomon had to carry out to satisfy God's expectations of the temple:

(a)   There were 183,300 laborers and overseers working on the temple (See 1 Kings 5) – represents the number of people the budget should care for.

(b)   A beginning date of building the temple was set – represents budget period.

(c)   The dimension of the temple was given – represents the quantifiable amount of the budget.

(d)   Porches and outside rooms were set – the elements of the budget.

(e)   Materials of the temple were given – elements of the budget.

(f)   Doors, stairs, and outside rooms around the temple were defined – elements of the budget.

(g)   Davidic covenant was confirmed to Solomon – elements of the budget.

(h)   The inside cedar walls were built – elements of the budget.

(i)   Dimensions and decorations of the Holy of Holies and the Holy place were given – elements of the budget.

(j)   Two cherubim in the Holy of Holies were identified – elements of the budget.

(k)   Wall and floor decorations were made – elements of the budget.

(l)   Doors of the Holy of Holies were created – elements of the budget.

(m)   The inner court was built – elements of the budget.

(n)   The temple was finished – budget adoption.

2) Secondly, Nehemiah said;

Then I told them of the hand of my God which was good upon me; as also the king's words that he had spoken unto me. And they said, Let us rise up and build. So they strengthened their hands for this good work.

(Nehemiah 2:18)

When building a budget, it is often foreseen that there would be resistance in terms of the dollars to be spent and the administration of those dollars. In the above scripture, Nehemiah described some of the challenges and opposition he had to overcome in order to get a functioning Jerusalem wall. When Nehemiah was informed of the ruins of the walls of Jerusalem, he immediately sought permission from the king to return back to Jerusalem to help building the wall.

In our lives, our financial situations might need a building up. And when that is the case, we obtain the right permission to help build our finances again. **This book talks about maturity after the recession. There was a recession meaning there was a falling wall in Jerusalem.** Nehemiah took upon himself as the budget manager and came to change the contrary circumstances.

Below is a list of obstacles he faced:

(a) In Nehemiah Chapter 5, Nehemiah discovered oppression.

(b) Nehemiah planned to stop oppression of the Jews.

(c) Nehemiah's plan was accepted and oppression stopped.

(d) Nehemiah's governed Judah for 12 years.

(e) Building of Jerusalem is hindered.

(f) Opposition by accusation.

(g) Accusation overcome by prayer and self-control.

(h) Opposition by treachery.

(i) Treachery overcome by prayer and bravery.

(j) Completion of the walls and gates of Jerusalem in 52 days.

(k) Effect of the finish work upon the Jews enemies.

(l) Treachery of many nobles of Judah.

(m) Change of governors and registration of inhabitants.

(n) Registration of the returned Jews from Babylon.

(o) The Levites returning from Babylon.

3) Thirdly, and lastly, Our Lord Jesus Christ managed His resources effectively.

There is a lad here, which hath five barley loaves, and two small fishes: but what are they among so many? ¹⁰*And Jesus said, Make the men sit down. Now there was much grass in the place. So the men sat down, in number about five thousand.* ¹¹*And Jesus took the loaves; and when he had given thanks, he distributed to the disciples, and the disciples to them that were set down; and likewise of the fishes as much as they would.* ¹²*When they were filled, he said unto his disciples, Gather up the fragments that remain, that nothing be lost.*

(John 6:9-12)

The above scripture shows the budgeting experience of Jesus Christ. When He embarked to feed the multitude, He needed to know the quantity of food on hand. They found five loaves and two fishes. But miraculously these were turned into more than 5,000 in loaves and fishes. Jesus was able to feed the 5,000 people with ease.

This means that Jesus was able to overcome His spending. After overcoming His spending, the Bible recalls there were fragments left. **Jesus was operating in a positive variance.** If you operate in a positive variance, then you would have performed exceptionally well. The Bible says, "God is in Christ, Christ is us", therefore if Jesus operates in positive variance we have no choice but to operate in such too.

Chapter 3 Review

1. God only rewards those who manage their affairs wisely. Hence, it is our responsibility to be good stewards of the resources He entrusts in our hands (Matthew 25:14-30).

2. As believers, it is imperative to carry out our duties, whether secular or spiritual with credibility and integrity. Let your yes be [a simple] yes, and your no be [a simple] no (James 5:12).

3. In order to have an effective budget, we must be cognizant of timing. This we can learn from ants, they have no overseer but they plan ahead of time, so that their future is well catered for (Proverbs 6:6-8).

4. We need money to live comfortably but the aspiration for more of it should not derail us from the will of God. Seeking God should be the paramount in our lives, because He has everything we need that pertain to life and godliness (Matthew 6:33).

5. When there was a falling wall in Jerusalem, Nehemiah took upon himself as the budget manager to change the contrary circumstances, so also are we to build our finances, now that the recession is over (Nehemiah 2:18).

(4)

Debt Management
&
Restructuring

Owe no man anything...

(Romans 13:8)

In this Chapter, you will learn about:

➢ Generation of Debtors

➢ Bible Teaching

➢ Avoidable Loans

➢ Arrest Bad Habits

➢ Debt Solutions

Managing your debt has to be one of the most important aspects of your finance. When you look and ask those around you, many will confess that they are almost buried in debt. We live in a society that thrives on borrowing and owing one another.

The system is built to encourage the recycling of money from one person to another and to the financial institutions. Through these practices, you become abused by debt. The purpose of this chapter is to help enlighten you and provide as much assistance about debt management.

GENERATION OF DEBTORS

Debt is when you owe other people and financial institutions. In the US, this appears to be the way of life. Everyone you see is mired in one form of debt. The sources of debt include student loans, unaffordable mortgages, expensive car notes, personal loans, payday loans, bank loans, etc. The failure to repay these loans would lead to adverse information being posted on your credit report.

You may not find this important right now, but on a day when you need the credit report to work in your favor, you will be informed of all the negative scores in it.

Therefore, it is important that you keep your debt under control so that you don't become overwhelmed. There are societies where personal debt is moderately managed; for instance in Nigeria, the use of cash to complete certain transactions is greatly encouraged. People do not walk around worried about piled up bills and creditors calling every single minute. Well that society is built in that way that you fit your coat according your size. You do not need to over extend yourself.

The US government is mired in debt. This is why there is a constant bickering between the Democrats and the Republicans. When the Clinton's Administration ended in 2000, the US had a surplus in its account. The economy was very good and personal debt was very low. The beginning of the Bush's administration brought an era of irresponsible spending that led to a blood - bath of deficits.

He engaged the US in two wars - Iraq and Afghanistan, based on faulty intelligence information. These wars cost money. Throughout his administration, the US was plunged in a sea of debt. This was inherited by President Barack Obama. And because President Bush ignored several or all domestic issues; nothing was done in the US to build and modernize infrastructures. As the new president assumed power, he decided to spend money in the US to modernize the infrastructures that were ignored eight years prior. Of course, there have been all types of criticisms levied against him, that he is spending too much money.

BIBLE TEACHING

The Bible is clear about debt – according to Apostle Paul "Owe no man" (Romans 13:8). When you owe others, they tend to mistreat you and make you serve as their slave. When you owe others, you are constantly praying for a way to pay them. When you see them coming, you either hide or pray that they do not bring up the issue.

Why then must you remain in bondage of that nature? Because of the debts at hand, you would let the phone ring forever, especially if it is the creditors calling. Follow the counsel of the apostle and owe no one.

AVOIDABLE LOANS

I found some information that could be useful in helping you to arrest your debt; but before expounding into details, let me address avoidable debts. It is important for you to avoid debts you can do without. For instance, if you are taking a college loan for your education, you must first seek other options before taking the loan.

There are many agencies that help students with grants and scholarships. You must do your research and pursue these channels before accepting a loan for your college or graduate school education. Asking for a college loan should be the absolute last option on your list. I have included 32 websites and company information for you to research and ask for grants and scholarships.

According to Jessica Ekhomu, 2008, in an email to me, she stated that "A large amount of scholarship money that has been set aside by companies for deserving minority students are either collecting dust or being returned to businesses because of a lack of interest. The following is a list of scholarships and their Web addresses to pass along to friends and family members with college-bound kids so that these free money will not go to waste".

(1)   Bell Labs Fellowships for under-represented minorities

http://www.bell-labs.com/

(2)   Student Inventors Scholarships

http://www.invent.org/collegiate/

(3)   Student Video Scholarships

http://www.christophers.org/vidcon2k.html

(4)   Coca-Cola Two-Year College Scholarships

http://www.coca-colascholars.org/programs.html

(5)   Holocaust Remembrance Scholarships
      http://holocaust.hklaw.com/

(6)   Ayn Rand Essay Scholarships
      http://www.aynrand.org/contests/

(7)   Brand Essay Competition
      http://www.instituteforbrandleadership.org/
      IBLEssayContest-2002Rules.htm

(8)   Gates Millennium Scholarships
      http://www.gmsp.org/nominationmaterials/
      read.dbm?ID=12

(9)   Xerox Scholarships for Students
      http://www2.xerox.com/go/xrx/about_xerox/
      about_xerox_detail.jsp

(10) Sports Scholarships and Internships
      http://www.ncaa.org/about/scholarships.html

(11) National Assoc. of Black Journalists Scholarships
      (NABJ)
      http://www.nabj.org/html/studentsvcs.html

(12) Saul T. Wilson Scholarships (Veterinary)
      http://www.aphis.usda.gov/mb/mrphr/jobs/stw.html

(13) Thurgood Marshall Scholarship Fund
      http://www.thurgoodmarshallfund.org/sk_v6.cfm

(14) FinAid: The Smart Students Guide to Financial
      Aid scholarships
      http://www.finaid.org< http://www.finaid.org/>

(15)　Presidential Freedom Scholarships
http://www.nationalservice.org/scholarships/

(16)　Microsoft Scholarship Program
http://www.microsoft.com/college/
scholarships/minority.asp

(17)　Wired Scholar Free Scholarship Search
http://www.wiredscholar.com/paying/
scholarship_search/pay_scholarship_se
http://www.wiredscholar.com/pag/scholarship_
search/pay_scholarship_se>

(18)　Hope Scholarships & Lifetime Credits
http://www.ed.gov/inits/hope/

(19)　William Randolph Hearst Endowed Scholarship
for Minority Students
http://www.apsanet.org/PS/grants/aspen3.cfm

(20)　Multiple List of Minority Scholarships
http://gehon.ir.miami.edu/financial-assistance/
Scholarship/black.html

(21)　Guaranteed Scholarships
http://www.guaranteed-scholarships.com/

(22)　Boeing Scholarships Program
http://www.boeing.com/companyoffices/
educationrelations/scholarships

(23)　Easley National Scholarship Program
http://www.naas.org/senior.htm

(24)   Maryland Artists Scholarships
       http://www.maef.org/

(25)   Jacki Tuckfield Memorial Graduate Business
       Scholarship (for AfrAm students in South Florida)
       http://www.jackituckfield.org/

(26)   Historically Black College & University
       Scholarships
       http://www.iesabroad.org/info/hbcu.htm

(27)   Actuarial Scholarships for Minority Students
       http://www.beanactuary.org/minority/
       scholarships.htm

(28)   International Students Scholarships & Aid Help
       http://www.iefa.org/

(29)   INROADS internships
       http://www.inroads.org/

(30)   ACT-SO "Olympics of the Mind" Scholarships
       http://www.naacp.org/work/actso/act-so.shtml

(31)   Black Alliance for Educational Options
       Scholarships
       http://www.baeo.org/options/privatelyfinanced.jsp

ARREST BAD HABITS

Bad habits are the worst. They can really lead you into debt. Many years ago, I was dealing with a bad habit and so I borrowed from my 401k, paycheck, even from individuals in order to support my habit. Bad habits are hard to break. I speak from experience. And so I do not condemn you struggling from one addiction or another. My prayers are with you. The apostle Paul wrote to the Galatians and us, saying;

Stand fast therefore in the liberty wherewith Christ hath made us free, and be not entangled again with the yoke of bondage.

(Galatians 5:1)

I admonish you to stand fast in your freedom. Your absolute freedom from addiction is certain. If you are struggling with ANY form of addiction, I highly suggest you commit this verse to memory. Post it on your refrigerator; post it in your bedroom and everywhere you can see and read it. It works. It really works...

The costs of bad habits could add up fast. You will find yourself in full denial and blame everyone and everything about your piling debt. If you used your paycheck to pay your bills, you will not have piling debts. A pastor once said to me "it is not how much money you make that matters, it is what you do with what you make."

He was so right. I made money but did not use it wisely. If you are reading this book on the plane, in your house, traveling, or anywhere; just stop and ask yourself, what can you drop today?

DEBT SOLUTIONS

Here is a list of debt management techniques I have compiled for you. I pray it works for you.

According to How To Directory (www.eHow.com) (2010), you should consider managing your personal debt in the following manner:

(1) Consolidate any student loans for lower payments. In most cases, consolidation brings down the interest rate on your older loans, but it also extends the time it takes for you to pay them off. There may be added benefits to consolidation if you do it during your grace period.

(2) List your average payments, and set up a personal budget. When you add up your expenses, it's always better to round amounts up and to set aside extra money than to come up short. Remember to include your living expenses, like rent, gas and electric bills, with your debt payments.

(3) Cut excess spending out of your lifestyle. There are simple ways to reduce your expenses, like making coffee at home in the morning instead of buying it on the way to work every day. Lots of little changes can lead to big savings over time.

(4) Get a credit card that matches your spending habits. If you want to have a month-to-month balance, you need a low-rate card, but if you pay your card off every month, you should look for one with low fees. You should avoid using a credit card as much as possible because it does add to your personal debt.

(5) Meet with a financial adviser. These counselors can help you create a long-term plan to get out of debt and stay out of it. Some non-profit groups have free debt counseling available to the public.

(6) You don't need to use a credit card to build good credit. Paying your student loans and telephone bill on time each month will build your credit ranking, without forcing you to take on new debt.

(7) You may want to set up your home to be more energy efficient to save on your electric bill. For example, compact, fluorescent light bulbs are a bit more expensive than regular ones, but they last

longer and use less energy, saving more in the long run.

(8) Avoid taking loans with low rates that increase dramatically after a few years.

(9) Don't spend more money than you make. Hold off on taking out an expensive, long-term loan to finance a new sports car until later in your career.

(10) Never get a new credit card with the sole intention of using it to manage your other debts (eHow.com, 2010).

According to Romance-fire, 2009, here are 15 Ways to Manage Your Money so You Can Clear Your Debt within a Year:

(1) Budget, Budget, Budget!

If you don't have a budget set in place to see what you have to pay and how much money you have, you will ultimately forget to pay certain people and spend more than you make. This will land you in trouble. Make a budget and stick to it.

(2) Work out a Payment Plan

With your debtors, whether they are your parents or banks, work out how you can pay them back so that you can still live properly. Negotiate lower interest rates and try to pay a bit more than you say you will pay per month to get on their good side. Set aside a percentage of your monthly income to go towards debts.

(3) Pay off the Smallest Debts First

This sounds a bit backwards, but if you try to pay off the bigger debts first, you are simply causing the smaller debts to build up interest and they will slowly become unmanageable. Rather pay off the smaller debts you have within a month or two and then with these out of the way, you can pay more to the bigger debts you have.

(4) Never Close Your Credit Cards

To keep your credit record high enough, don't close your credit cards. Rather put them away and don't use them. Once they are paid off, just keep them aside without using them until you have cleared the rest of your debts.

(5) Consolidate Your Debt

Debt consolidation can only help if you have accounts and loans which are in arrears and you are paying a lot in terms of interest. The point of consolidating this debt is to lower the amount you pay by making several interest costs into one smaller one. It can also greatly reduce the installment you have to pay each month while also getting rid of debt collectors phoning you all the time.

For money you have borrowed from family, never use debt consolidation because you don't have interest to pay them anyway (hopefully). If you do, rather work out another agreement.

(6) Pay more than the Installment

This can be easier said than done and if you have a large installment already, paying more than you owe will seem impossible. You should try where you can, especially with the bigger loans, to pay more even if it means sacrificing a night out at a restaurant to get an extra little bit to pay.

(7) Cut Down on Your Expenses

Most of the time, people try to pay off their debts while still living the same way. If you really want to be successful in clearing your debt within a year, you will have to relook at your lifestyle and what you spend each month. Avoid expensive payday loan lenders with too high interest. You must try to cut down as much as you can to have extra money for paying accounts and debts.

Eat at home more, only go out once a month instead of four times, don't go on shopping sprees and perhaps even find a cheaper place to live, get a cheaper car or get an extra job.

(8) Plan Ahead

With debts you have to worry about, the last thing on your mind will be opening health care plans and retirement plans, but all these things should not be left just because you have debts. You must work extra hard to pay your debts and for these policies because they are so important. Planning ahead like this will also force you to save more money each month and when you are debt free, you will have a lot extra to place into these policies.

(9) Living Costs

When you have a lot of money to pay back to family or to a bank, it is advisable to go rent a relatively small apartment within your financial means. It is very easy to say "don't worry it will be fine" and choose a nice house somewhere with a garden and a pool, but if you have debts and cannot really afford this, then choose a smaller, cheaper place for now. You can always move into a bigger place when you are debt free in a year's time and can afford it.

(10) Be Self Sufficient

Many people have gone green and started planting their own vegetables and fruits. While this is green and helps you to be healthier and avoid diseases like cancer, it can also save you money a lot and may be a perfect way to clear your debts. By growing your own produce, you don't need to starve yourself or give up eating healthy food because you cannot afford it. This will allow you to eat properly and save lots of money on your grocery bill.

(11) Natural Remedies

In the same note, you can also look at more natural ways to cure illnesses and help with ailments which are far cheaper than medicine. You can even use natural products as skin care products which will save a lot of money and may actually be safer and healthier for your skin. Things like oatmeal and sage help fight pimples. It has also been discovered and tested over the years that garlic is the best defense against colds and flu.

(12) Exercise

One way to become debt free easily is to cut down on the so called luxuries like your gym membership. You also don't want to give in, because in so doing, you become unfit and unhealthy, so here is the best solution. Instead of driving your car which costs a lot in gas, rather walk or cycle. This will allow you to cancel your gym membership.

So you can cut out on two expenses and still get fit and keep trim.

(13) Household Items

While you want to have a nice home with all the latest gadgets and furniture, becoming debt free requires you make some sacrifices. One of the best ways to get some extra cash is to have a yard sale. While many newly married couples do not have much to begin with, there are sometimes lots of old items that come into a marriage that can be sold. Maybe you have some old toys or gifts from ex boyfriends or girlfriends that you can sell, or perhaps you both have furniture already and you need to get rid of the double items. You can sell these items to second hand shops or online to make more money and clear out your home.

(14) Shop Mathematically

When you buy food or clothes or anything for your home, make sure you always work out how much you can spend and keep a calculation of this while you are at the shops. In fact, to make sure you don't spend more than you are supposed to, only take the exact amount of cash with you that you have worked out. This will avoid the shock when you realize that you have overspent on your groceries. This will also teach you to shop economically too and look for the cheapest items that will also last the longest.

(15) Reward Yourself

Like anything in life, when we reward ourselves, we are more motivated to continue doing what we have set out to do. The same goes for clearing your debts, and once you have solved your debt problem in one area; give yourself a small reward for doing so well. Then go on to conquer the next debt you have.

[Wishing you all the best] in becoming debt free in a year" (Romance-fire, 2009).

Chapter 4 Review

1. The Bible admonishes us to keep out of debt and owe no man anything, except to love one another. By this, we are not under any obligation to please people but to sincerely love them with no strings attached (Romans 13:8).

2. You are made free in Christ Jesus and are not to be in bondage to anything, therefore deal with any bad habit that wants to hinder your financial life (Galatians 5:1).

3. Cut down on your expenses and live within your means. Adjust your lifestyle and live one day at a time (Proverbs 28:20).

4. Budget for your desired glorious future and trust God who can surpass your financial plan (Proverbs 24:3-4).

5. Endeavor to get out of debt if you do not want to be servant for the rest of your life (Proverbs 22:7).

(5)

Philanthropy

...Remember the words of the Lord Jesus, how he said, It is more blessed to give than to receive.

(Acts 20:35)

In this Chapter, you will learn about:

➤ Religious Philanthropy

➤ Spiritual Horizon of Philanthropy

➤ Faith-guided Philanthropy

After the recession, you need to indulge in philanthropic activities. Here is why. There are several people who were hit hard by the recession; more than likely they have not been able to fully recover, as such they need a hand from you. There are heavenly and earthly rewards for being philanthropic. This chapter will address the impact of philanthropy during economic downturn or a recession.

People who are generally philanthropic in nature and guided by their faith could occasionally be affected financially by the global economic turmoil. When these economic ills persist, philanthropy becomes a hard practice due to the fact that there is less to give. A philanthropist enjoys giving. That is their way of life.

Their overall attitude of giving is that it provides an intrinsic satisfaction to the philanthropist because of their involvement in a good deed. Most people who participate in philanthropic activities are generally motivated by their faith. According to Eikenberry (2006), philanthropy is "the act of giving money and other resources, including time, to aid individuals, causes, and charitable organizations (Philanthropy, 2000, p. 590).

Philanthropy is important to religious organizations because it serves as the life source for their natural existence, outside of any supernatural consideration.

This chapter reviews the impact of philanthropy when there is an economic downturn or a recession. Let me note that that giving grants a lively impetus to the local assembly by ensuring that it is functioning properly in the daily operations and in meeting necessary obligations with regards to going concern requirements.

When philanthropic giving decreases, religious organizations are affected by various economic woes - such as inability for Ministries to support their local branch pastors or religious leaders; local school projects are abandoned and school children are disenfranchised; the employed janitor is laid off and becomes a statistic in the large unemployment pool; immediate issues such as mortgage payments and essential church services are threatened because of the decrease in philanthropic giving.

RELIGIOUS PHILANTHROPY

According to Bentley (2002), there is a historic and a rich tradition of philanthropy. He notes that philanthropic teaching relates to passing the act of philanthropy to the next generation. He noted that "religious philanthropy typically is an act of "voluntary" giving or service on behalf of a higher divine authority" (Bentley, 2002).

This supports the notion that the act of giving is either divinely ordained or it is driven by intrinsic motivation of generosity. Bentley discusses the best age to teach philanthropy. This is important because those who learn philanthropy at an early age tend to practice it throughout their lives.

Bentley (2002) also writes, "Studies suggest that caring and sharing can be taught at all ages" (Bentley and Nissan, 1996). This learning begins very early. Infants can exhibit empathic behavior within the first few years of life. Bentley's assertion supports the notion that what children learned at a very young age carries on throughout their lives.

Growing up, my mom would ensure that when we got to church, she'd give us money for the offertory period. She made sure that we did not miss the giving part of the church service. She was very passionate about giving because that was her foremost ministry. That was her purpose in life – to give to others and bless them as much as possible. When we did not have a lot of money to give in church, she made sure we put in the possible minimum in the offering bucket as if to say we were being marked for attendance. Years later, I am greatly enlightened by this type of ministry; the ministry of benevolence, better known as philanthropy. It is widely discussed and encouraged in the Bible.

Apostle Paul towards the end of his third missionary journey, enjoined the elders in Miletus about giving.

The Scripture says;

I have showed you all things, how that so laboring ye ought to support the weak, and to remember the words of the Lord Jesus, how he said, It is more blessed to give than to receive.

(Acts 20:35)

Paul took the ministry of giving to another level. He implored the elders that giving has to be an essential and integral part of their life. On this note, he challenged them to see the blessing behind giving, noting that it is better to give than to receive. Apostle Paul's admonition was just one amongst many in the Bible that talked about the art of giving.

In his letter to the Hebrews, Paul wrote that;

For God [is] not unrighteous to forget your work and labor of love, which ye have showed toward his name, in that ye have ministered to the saints, and do minister.

(Hebrews 6:10)

To be philanthropic is to show a labor of love especially when there seems to be famine in the land. God understands and sees the sacrificial giving that the philanthropist gives during hard times. To encourage the saints, the Lord informs the philanthropist that their labor of love is not forgotten and would be rewarded. When a giver gives, he really gives unto the Lord by faith because he knows that the Lord would reward him.

In Psalms 41:1-3, King David talked about the benefits of remembering the poor in time of need.

He stated:

Blessed is he that considereth the poor: the LORD will deliver him in time of trouble. ²The LORD will preserve him, and keep him alive; and he shall be blessed upon the earth: and thou wilt not deliver him unto the will of his enemies. ³The LORD will strengthen him upon the bed of languishing: thou wilt make all his bed in his sickness.

If there is any doubt in your mind about being philanthropic, these verses should encourage you. Bentley notes that families that practice any form of philanthropy have the tendencies of passing the act of generosity to the generation that follows.

He writes;

"This early or primordial learning occurs primarily in the home. Children learn empathy by being cared for and by taking care of others. They experience this from their parents, family members, and neighbors. Today, many more children rely on sources outside the home, such as day care providers or messages they see in books, on videos, and on television (Bentley, 2002, Page 26)".

Furthermore, Bentley (2002) mentioned some examples of "common religious beliefs that distinguish religious philanthropy from other types of giving include..." (Page 22)

- Viewing God as the ultimate authority - Bentley holds the view that religious philanthropists see their deeds as driven by a higher authority; as such there is an obligation to follow through with the instructions from above.

- Viewing oneself as a steward - The "hard core" philanthropist sees their role as that of a steward - which is to say that it is a "calling" which needs a response.

- Giving as a way to thank God - There is another group of philanthropists that believe that "giving back" is a way of thanking God for what He has done for them.

- Giving a fair share - Bentley notes that another group of philanthropist believes that giving is a way of paying their "fair share" to the society which they belong to.

SPIRITUAL HORIZON OF PHILANTHROPY

This angle of philanthropy is almost similar to the faith-guided approach to philanthropy. Schervish presents a unique look at the spiritual perspective mixed with a business dimension. He wrote that;

"The spiritual aspect of the supply side and draw out implications for tax policy and fundraising that derive from the analysis" (Schervish, 2000, Page 20).

This discussion centers on the fact that the philanthropist is able to take advantage of tax conditions which are favorable to the giver. From a spiritual perspective, the giver looks at the fact that their giving has enabled their spiritual life. Scherivish wrote about the inclination model - In the inclination model, wealth holders tend to give very large or substantial gifts to charity; such as the story of the Bill and Melinda Gates Foundation. Their giving shows a great degree of care and spiritual insinuations.

Schervish (2000) stated that;

"Several inclinations of wealth holders that dispose them to make substantial gifts to charity. The implications of the supply-side analysis for advancing a discernment approach to fundraising and for the repeal of the estate tax" (Page 17).

FAITH-GUIDED PHILANTHROPY

Esposito and Foote (2002) provided some philanthropic experiences guided by faith. The authors enlisted the initial questions that are asked by philanthropist before embarking on their charitable mission. They stated that;

"Donors of faith may find themselves facing profound questions: What does my religion teach about charity? How can faith-guided giving become a family enterprise? How can we support worthy but distinctly sectarian nonprofit organizations or causes?" (Page 16).

Esposito and Foote (2002) stated that the philanthropic family would pose these questions in their own way;

"Cast in terms of their own cultural, ethnic, and family traditions as well as their experiences in coming to faith" (Page 16).

In this example, the authors show the attitude portrayed in African American setting;

"Betty and Jean Fairfax do not distinguish between the spiritual-based African American philanthropy and the struggle for justice and equality. They give both to their church and to the struggle. In African American churches, it is not unusual to see two collections on Sunday service, one for the church and one for a young person ready to head off for college but short of funds" (Page 19-20).

This example is very real in the sense that the African American community continues to be a close knit group whereby, they pull one another up, especially where there seems to be hardship. Esposito and Foote (2002) ended their article by stating that;

"Faith-guided family grant making has much in common with secular family grant making - choosing and funding a giving vehicle, marshalling family support for the enterprise, selecting grantees, and managing office and assets. But for families of faith, the connection with their spiritual life adds a meaningful extra dimension" (Page 21).

This happens in many faith-based churches, and it pushes for greater philanthropic endeavors.

Faith guided philanthropy in African American churches: Esposito and Foote (2002) gave a compelling illustration of practical philanthropy guided by faith in the African-American churches. For instance, monies are collected in order to support the educational endeavors of a youth at the church.

Belief in tithe and offerings: Esposito and Foote (2002) noted that practicing Christians believe in the concept of tithes and offerings. They believe that there is a mandate from God to ensure that portions of their income would be giving to the church, based specifically on their faith.

Philanthropic giving other than cash: Esposito and Foote (2002) stated that other philanthropists believe in giving property other than cash. These philanthropists give paintings, land, buildings, arts, etc. in place of cash.

Each of the themes discussed shows that philanthropy is heralded by the passion exemplified by the philanthropist. The unfortunate case of economic downturn affects a vast number of people and organizations. Where there is instability, it becomes very difficult to embrace philanthropy. When a nation suffers recession, progress in every area is impeded.

Religious organizations are not immune to recession problems, the church ends up laying off people, and unable to render basic benevolent assistance. The parishioners become more self-absorbed in trying to solve their own economic ill before supporting the church. The teaching of religious philanthropy and faith-guided philanthropy almost seem to disappear into the air because the economic decisions facing the philanthropist appear greater than giving.

Chapter 5 Review

1. Philanthropists take delight in giving because they believe that the more they give, the more they are empowered to reach out to more people (Proverbs 11:24-25).

2. Humanitarians who are guided by their faith give generously to those going through financial difficulties. They know that the Lord will preserve them in times of their challenges (Psalm 41:1-3).

3. It is more blessed to give than to receive because in so doing, we heap up and store for ourselves treasures in heaven, where neither moth nor rust nor worm consume and destroy (Acts 20:35).

4. Keep up the good work of being a worthy ambassador of God on earth. Remember, God is not unrighteous to forget your labor of love and He will reward you in due season (Hebrews 6:10).

5. God is able to make all grace come to you in abundance, so that you always have sufficiency in all things, but the level of grace you experience depends on the degree of your cheerful giving (2 Corinthians 9:6-8).

(6)

Contingency

Make haste, O God, to deliver me; make haste to help me, O
LORD

(Psalm 70:1)

In this Chapter, you will learn about:

> ➤ Nature of Contingency

> ➤ Joseph and his Generation

> ➤ Pharaoh's Dilemma

> ➤ Burial in Nigeria

> ➤ The Value of Contingency

> ➤ Planning Contingently

NATURE OF CONTINGENCY

Contingency is a synonymous word for emergency. A contingent situation arises without warning or a form of caution. It normally springs up without any formal announcement. No wonder the Bible says;

Behold, I will do a new thing; now it shall spring forth; shall ye not know it? I will even make a way in the wilderness [and] rivers in the desert.

(Isaiah 43:19)

That springing forth is normally not planned for. It is an incident that would catch everyone unprepared. When Prophet Isaiah proclaimed those words, he intended to warm the children of Israel that the move of God would be sudden. In that same verse, a closer examination of it shows that God appeared to be a bit impatient with the reader.

Because the Word of God says, *"shall ye not know it?"* Someone in the midst of emergency normally does not plan for it. Emergency springs forth without any warning. In situations whereby you are not properly prepared, you would find yourself struggling.

In this chapter, I plan to share some wisdom on contingency planning.

In 2008, the United States started to feel financial pressures all around. The debt level was high. There was an administration that appeared clueless about what to do. The following catastrophes persisted:

- Financial institutions were folding up.
- Homes were being foreclosed upon.
- Unemployment was running away wild.
- Families were feeling the pinch and were hurting bad.
- Cars were being repossessed.
- Bank accounts were being shut down.

JOSEPH AND HIS GENERATION

The story of Joseph is a fascinating story. In many churches, this story is being told over and over again. Jacob later known as Israel loved his son Joseph so much that he bought him a coat of multiple colors. The meaning of the colors represents the Glory of God which radiates in our lives.

Ask ye of the Lord rain in the time of the latter rain; so the Lord shall make bright clouds, and give them showers of rain, to every one grass in the field.

(Zechariah 10:1)

In that same verse, the Prophet declared that the Lord shall make bright clouds.

Jacob understood the concept of bright clouds. So, he bought his son, Joseph, a coat of many colors, which represents bright clouds. Joseph needed to learn wisdom. **A man seeking contingency plan needs wisdom.** The way Joseph got his wisdom was his ability to deal with his brothers. Joseph was naïve when he told his brothers the dreams he had. As a result, he went through a process that matured him to properly handle subsequent divine information.

Many people's dreams were terminated because those dreams were prematurely made public without adequate preparation. And it's not everyone that is happy about your dream. This is evidence by the envy displayed by Joseph's brothers. The story goes on to say Joseph was abandoned in a pit and eventually sold. The beauty of this experience was that the sale of Joseph was a necessary step for his destiny.

Now Joseph found himself in Egypt. His ministry started there. The Bible teaches us to flee all appearances of evil (1 Thessalonians 5:22). Joseph found favor in the sight of Potiphar but the enemy had a different agenda for his life.

And it came to pass after these things, that his master's wife [Potiphar's wife] cast her eyes upon Joseph; and she said, Lie with me."

(Genesis 39:7, Emphasis Mine)

The maturation of Joseph was the birth of his wisdom. When Potiphar's wife made a pass at Joseph, wisdom prevailed and Joseph fled from the scene. Because of his diligence and prudence, Potiphar's wife took advantage of his innocence and lied about the occurrence of the events that truly transpired.

And she caught him by his garment saying, Lie with me: and he left his garment in her hand, and fled, and got him out.

(Genesis 39:12)

Joseph was thrown in jail. The imprisonment of Joseph was vital for his ascension to the throne. The apostle Paul was jailed and released. All the apostles were jailed and released. Prophet Jeremiah was jailed and released. The imprisonment of Joseph was no different from any of these giants in the Bible. In each case, there was an encounter with the Lord in the jail. Joseph had an encounter with the Lord. This encounter led him to be a deep interpreter of dreams such, just as Daniel did while he was in captivity in Babylon (Read Genesis chapter 40).

Joseph befriended two of his fellow inmates. One was the baker and the other was the butler. Joseph skillfully interpreted their dreams. The dream by the chief butler was the key to Joseph's destiny. When Joseph effectively interpreted the dream of the chief butler, he made a covenant with him that he should remember him upon his release.

Yet did not the chief butler remember Joseph, but forgot him.

(Genesis 40:23)

Although this scripture reflects the butler's forgetfulness of the covenant with Joseph, it is clear that the timing was not in alignment with God's divine timing, and so, when it mattered the most, the chief butler remembered Joseph.

PHARAOH'S DILEMMA

And it came to pass in the morning, that his spirit was troubled; and he sent and called for all the magicians of Egypt, and all the wise men thereof: and Pharaoh told them his dream; but there was none that could interpret them unto Pharaoh. ⁹Then spake the chief butler unto Pharaoh, saying, I do remember my faults this day:

(Genesis 41:8-9)

The dream Pharaoh had was a dream that inspired the era of contingency. Pharaoh had a dream that showed leanness of famine in the land. In that same dream, he saw prosperity too. The dream was made clear because Joseph divinely interpreted it. When the chief butler came to Pharaoh, he apologized for his forgetfulness and asked for repentance and then brought to his attention, the man of destiny.

Pharaoh jumped at the request to allow Joseph to interpret his dream. Since all the magicians, astrologers, soothsayers, divinators could not interpret the dream, Joseph had to step in to fulfill his destiny. Joseph described the era of contingency to Pharaoh. He was able to interpret the complicated dream in accordance to God's precepts.

Joseph drew out a plan. This plan showed or reflected the ability to operate under emergency. Pharaoh was so impressed by Joseph's keenness and wisdom that he elevated him immediately to become the Project Manager. A Project Manager is a person who handles the administration, the planning, the designing, and the execution of a project.

King Pharaoh needed a project manager and as a result, Joseph was chosen. Joseph now designed how to get the nation out of famine by employing contingent values. He planned such that there would be enough for Egypt and the neighboring nations. Even the following folks enjoyed the blessing in Joseph's life - Jebusites, Edomites, Ammonites, Moabites. The morale of the story is that everyone enjoys the blessing of contingency, even the man's enemies. The reason for this is because the contingent blessing is not a selfish blessing.

BURIAL IN NIGERIA

Several Nigerians live abroad and because of this, they normally will get the news about their ailing parents When their parents pass away, the burden of the burial falls on their shoulders; somehow it is believed that the Nigerian in America has money to fund the ceremony. So they are asked to bring lots of money, and I mean lots! This could be a problem because if the individual does not have emergency money, it could create a lot of stress for them.

The stress can create family problems because an individual who is married to an American would want to spend some money which has not been budgeted for his parent's burial. And the American does not see the wisdom in all that spending. As a result of cultural difference, the American does not see the rational for that spending. Normally, this would create unneeded tension in the house.

This could even lead to divorce or separation. The stress from not having money for this type of burial can lead to some health issues. For instance, stress can cause high blood pressure, anxiety, depression, oppression. These types of illnesses can lead to untimely death of this individual. The third point of view to this is financial woes. The burial cost that has not been planned for, could lead a man to bankruptcy.

The person who has not been able to pay his basic bills or basic expenditures would find it extremely difficult to come up with a huge lump sum amount for a family burial. If they divert their pay checks to this cause, their utility bills will be unpaid, their mortgages or rent, automobile costs, and possibly insurance could be cancelled. As a result of this, it is important to know and see the importance of contingency planning.

THE VALUE OF CONTINGENCY

The story of Joseph in Genesis 39 and 40 showed how he project managed Egypt from chaos to prosperity. Following the same framework, here are some advantages or values of contingent planning:

(1) *Contingency allows for a proper accountability of expenditures:* This means that when you plan contingently and when the day of use comes, all the expenditures can be properly accounted for. And all the budgetary items would be under proper control.

(2) *Contingency planning ensures that deficit nature is avoided:* The reason the United States government is dealing now with a lot of debt is because of the lack of contingency planning in the Bush administration. The mess in the Bush administration spilled over, creating more deficit than ever known. The Bush administration claimed that the deficit was a result of the wars in Iraq and Afghanistan.

That's true, but the fact remains that there was no contingency planning in place. The essence of this chapter is to encourage people to become contingent planners.

(3) *Contingency planning brings joy to family, Hallelujah!!!*: I believe that when the family agrees to contingently plan, the amount they set aside on a monthly basis is no longer missed by the family, so therefore, on a rainy day, instead of running helter skelter looking for monies to borrower, the family can easily walk into the contingency account and withdraw what they need. There is no stress involved.

(4) *Contingency planning can increase your life*: Every night the individual will sleep well.

According to Psalm 127:2;

It is vain for you to rise up early, to sit up late, to eat the bread of sorrows: for so he giveth the beloved sleep.

I believe contingency planning is of the Lord. Thus, it is imperative to take our contingency account to God and let him know why. Contingency planning breeds good sleep as stated in this scripture; at night the individual will sleep like a baby, and have no care of this world because they know if they receive that emergency call, they are able to react accordingly.

(5) *Contingency planning is a form of blessing:* A blessed man is the one who knows how to save up for a rainy day. It is ungodly to live from paycheck to paycheck. We need to consider our ways and change this slavery mindset. Living from one paycheck to another paycheck is nothing but an impoverished way of life. (See the chapter on Maximization of Income)

PLANNING CONTINGENTLY

The model presented by Joseph in the act of planning contingently works on a large scale project. Remember, Joseph was planning for his adopted nation and the surrounding nations. This means that he was planning for his friends and enemies.

The Bible teaches in the Book of Romans 12:17-21;

Recompense to no man evil for evil. Provide things honest in the sight of all men. [18]If it be possible, as much as lieth in you, live peaceably with all men. [19]Dearly beloved, avenge not yourselves, but rather give place unto wrath: for it is written, Vengeance is mine; I will repay, saith the Lord. [20]Therefore, if thine enemy hunger, feed him; if he thirst, give him drink: for in so doing thou shalt heap coals of fire on his hear. [21]Be not overcome of evil, but overcome evil with good.

In this passage of scripture, it is clear that Joseph was applying *Godly* principles by ensuring his planning would take care of even the surrounding nations. Joseph knew what *Godly* deeds were and he knew that when enemy nations would come to Egypt, they would have to be kind to them.

Here are some principles to follow:

(1) *Plan with your enemy in mind:* What you do for your enemy, God will do for you. Whatever you do to those who despitefully use you, the Lord who is a rewarder of all forms and shapes of good deeds will do the same to you.

Similarly, make sure you plan for friends. In a time of famine, friendship or enemy cannot be easily distinguished because *famine is famine.* Therefore, a wise man who contingently plans would be able to cover the spectrum of people he comes into contact with.

(2) *Allow a family consensus to drive the dollar amount being saved up for contingency:* When there is family agreement about a direction of what needs to be saved, such direction is blessed by God. Families need to work more closely together in one accord.

And when the day of Pentecost was fully come, they were all with **one accord** *in one place.* [2] *And suddenly there came a sound from heaven as of a rushing mighty wind, and it filled all the house where they were sitting.*

(Acts 2:1-2)

One accord creates the release of the supernatural blessing.

(3) *Use the 10% rule for contingency planning:* I am going to assume that you already pay 10% of your income as tithes to God; now you should pay 10% to your contingency account. Once you make a practice of that, before you know it, the contingency account will become bulky. Whatever you give to the church should match your contingency account.

(4) *Lump sum approach:* In this approach, the individual involved might come into contact with a blessing of a large sum of money. Instead of spending up every dime, he can put away 50% of that for contingency reasons. Remember that any side project does not have any constancy in it. So, when it comes in once every six months, or once in every year, the individual should discipline himself or herself enough to put aside 50% for contingency reasons.

(5) *The April Rule*: The premise for the April rule is that during the month of April, most people file their income taxes. Someone without a contingency method should try employing this methodology. Whatever tax refund they receive should go towards their contingency account. Note that all through the year, the government has been taking money from their paychecks, so the government is serving as the contingency custodian. During the tax season, they can now request their tax refund which will now become the contingency account.

Chapter 6 Review

1. Contingency planning can increase your life span and bring joy to your family. Unless God builds the house, they labor in vain who build it, and because of this, trust God and walk in accordance to His plans (Psalm 127:1-2).

2. There is a general belief that someone somewhere has all the money to fund emergency ceremonies. As an adept practitioner of the covenant, endeavor to be rooted and built up in Christ, and follow not after the tradition of men (Colossians 2:8).

3. When there is family agreement about a direction of what needs to be saved, such course is blessed by God. Families need to work more closely together in one accord. The power of togetherness is not easily be broken (Psalm 133, Acts 2:1-2).

4. Joseph went through a process that matured him to properly handle divine information. This was necessary because he naïvely shared his dreams with his brothers. Protect your dream and share with the right people at the right time (Genesis 37: 5-20, Matthew 10:36).

5. God who makes all things beautiful in His time remembered Joseph at the appointed time, even though the chief butler forgot him for two years. Do not give up on your dreams because God is in control (Ecclesiastes 3:11, Genesis 40:23).

Epilogue

I believe this book has helped with transforming some of your thoughts regarding your finances. There may be areas in which you already manage your finances well, if that's the case, there would be no need to change your approach, just improve it. And I compliment your effort a great deal. If you have not worked as hard in your finances, tomorrow is too late to start. You need to start today.

Concepts such as budgeting could be implemented immediately for you to monitor and control spending patterns. Even as I write today, Sunday, July 31, 2011, the United States Congress is knotted in a gridlock of how to manage the national debt. There's a great debate on debt ceiling going on. As the country gets serious about her debt, so should you. Carrying a load of unnecessary debt deters you from doing other meaningful things in life.

Finally, let your resourcefulness create room for you and others. Explore reasonable and strategic ways to generate income for yourself and your family. As you do that, remember that you are to minister to others too.

Serve as a divine ladder to someone else; as you do, blessings will continuously flow in your direction. I'll see you in the next book. Before that, pray my strength in the Lord your God waxes strong, as I continue to "look unto Jesus" (Hebrews 12:2).

REFERENCES

Bentley, R. J. (2002). Speaking to a higher authority: Teaching philanthropy in religious settings. *New Directions for Philanthropic Fundraising*, 2002(36), 21-36. Retrieved from EBSCO*host* on January 10, 2011 from http://ezproxy.library.capella.edu/login?url=http://search.ebscohost.com/login.aspx?direct=true&db=bth&AN=10648337&site=ehost-live&scope=site

Eikenberry, A. M. (2008). Fundraising in the new philanthropy environment: The benefits and challenges of working with giving circles. *Nonprofit Management & Leadership*, 19(2), 141-152. doi:10.1002/nml.212; Retrieved on January 10, 2011 from http://ezproxy.library.capella.edu/login?url=http://search.ebscohost.com/login.aspx?direct=true&db=bth&AN=35809778&site=ehost-live&scope=site

Esposito, V. M., & Foote, J. (2002). Faith and family philanthropy: Stories of giving from faith-guided family grant makers. *New Directions for Philanthropic Fundraising*, 2002(35), 15-22. Retrieved from EBSCO*host* on January 10, 2011 from http://ezproxy.library.capella.edu/login?url=http://search.ebscohost.com/login.aspx?direct=true&db=bth&AN=10648329&site=ehost-live&scope=site

eHow.com (2010). How to Manage Personal Debt, Retrieved on April 1, 2011, from http://www.ehow.com/how_2076640_manage-personal-debt.html#ixzz1KI0bXcF6

Romance-fire (2009). "15 Ways to Manage Your Money so You Can Clear Your Debt within a Year", retrieved on April 1, 2011, from http://www.romance-fire.com/2009/01/30/15-ways-to-manage-your-money-so-you-can-clear-your-debt-within-a-year/

Schervish, P. G. (2000). The spiritual horizons of philanthropy: New directions for money and motives. *New Directions for Philanthropic Fundraising*, 2000(29), 17-32. Retrieved from EBSCO*host* on January 10, 2011 from http://ezproxy.library.capella.edu/login?url=http://search.ebscohost.com/login.aspx?direct=true&db=bth&AN=10648281&site=ehost-live&scope=site

Watson, G. (2010). Entrepreneurship, Education, and Ethics, Definition of Entrepreneurship, Retrieved on October 26, 2010, from http://www.gregwatson.com/entrepreneurship-definition/

Mintzberg, H., Alhstrand, B., and Lampel, J. (1998). Strategy Safari, Free Press

Lehr, C. (1980). How 3M develops entrepreneurial spirit throughout the organization.

Management Review, *69*(10), 31. Retrieved from Business Source Complete database.http://ezproxy.library. capella.edu/login?url=http://search.ebscohost.com/ login.aspx?direct=true&db=bth&AN=6267651&site =ehost-live&scope=site

Lemberg, P. (2002). Nine Entrepreneurial Mistakes that Can Kill Your Organization.*Nonprofit World*, *20*(3), 14-16. Retrieved from Business Source Complete database. http://ezproxy.library.capella.edu/login?url=http:// search.ebscohost.com/login.aspx?direct=true&db =bth&AN=19072247&site=ehost-live&scope=site

Gisonni, D. (2002). "How to Ignite Entrepreneurial Spirit in Your Organization"

Nonprofit World, *20*(5), 23-25. Retrieved from Business Source Complete database.http:// ezproxy.library.capella.edu/login?url=http:// search.ebscohost.com/login.aspx?direct=true&db =bth&AN=19072274&site=ehost-live&scope=site

Hisrich, R. D., Peters, M., and Shepherd, D. A. (2005). Entrepreneurship, 6 Edition. New York: McGraw-Hill Irwin,http://www.sbaer.uca.edu/publications/ entrepreneurship/pdf/11.pdf

PRAYER TO RECEIVE SALVATION

In order to start a productive relationship with God and continually walk in victory, you must surrender your life to the Lordship of Jesus Christ. If you have not accepted Jesus Christ as your Lord and Savior, I encourage you to pray the following prayer aloud in order to receive your salvation.

Dear Lord Jesus, I have finally decided today to surrender my life to you. I believe with my heart and confess with my mouth that you died for my sins and that you were raised from the dead for my justification. I confess all my sins and ask you to cleanse me in your blood. I receive the gift of salvation by faith in the precious name of Jesus Christ.

I congratulate you for the prayer you have just prayed because you have just made the most important decision in life. Welcome to the loving family of God and may the Lord God bless and uphold you to fulfill your purpose on earth in the name of Jesus.

I will like to hear from you. I can be reached through my address stated at the end of the book.

ABOUT THE AUTHOR

Godfrey Ekhomu is a Certified Public Accountant. He is currently working on his doctoral degree in Organization and Management. He works as a freelance consultant backed by several years of business experience with large and small scale organizations. His roles have been strategic and tactical in nature. He presently resides in the Chicagoland area.

In his spiritual vocation, Pastor Godfrey heads up the internationally renowned Telephone Bible Study Ministry - TBSM. He is affiliated with Glorious Church of the First Born - Benue State, Nigeria, and KingsWord International Church - Chicago, USA. He stands on the promise of Hebrews 12:2; "Looking unto Jesus."

TO CONTACT US

For more information on how to develop a healthy relationship with Jesus Christ, you can send me an email.

Email Address:

gekhomu@aol.com

To order more copies of this book or other inspiring books

Visit

www.gkscrybes.com

WATCH OUT! THE FOLLOWING BOOKS ARE TO BE RELEASED SHORTLY BY THE AUTHOR

1. Accountability

2. Looking Unto Jesus in 366 Days (A Daily Devotion)

GOE ENTERPRISES

FINANCIAL CONSULTANTS

P. O. BOX 2661, NORTHLAKE, IL
60164

(708).516.5259

SEVERAL YEARS OF BUSINESS
EXPERTISE TO HELP YOU

TBSM

Telephone Bible Study Ministry

Every Thursday Night
At 8:00PM (CST)

712.432.0180, Access 134876

TBSM123 @gmail.com
(708). 516.5259

Looking Unto Jesus – Hebrews 12:2